Loren Eiseley

Twayne's United States Authors Series

Warren French, Editor
Indiana University, Indianapolis

TUSAS 442

LOREN EISELEY
(1907–1977)
Photograph courtesy of Frank Ross

Loren Eiseley

By Andrew J. Angyal

Elon College

Twayne Publishers • Boston

Loren Eiseley

Andrew J. Angyal

Copyright © 1983 by G.K. Hall & Company
All Rights Reserved
Published by Twayne Publishers
A Division of G. K. Hall & Company
70 Lincoln Street
Boston, Massachusetts 02111

Book Production by Marne B. Sultz

Book Design by Barbara Anderson

Printed on permanent/durable acid-free
paper and bound in the United States of
America.

Library of Congress Cataloging in
Publication Data

Angyal, Andrew J.
Loren Eiseley.

(Twayne's United States authors series;
TUSAS 442)
Bibliography: p. 134
Includes index.
1. Eiseley, Loren C., 1907–1977—
Criticism and interpretation.
I. Title. II. Series.
PS3555.I78Z54   1983   818'.5409
82-25483
ISBN 0-8057-7381-9

For Jennifer

Contents

About the Author

The natural history writer has interested Andrew J. Angyal from the time he first read Thoreau in high school. He became an admirer of Loren Eiseley after being introduced to his works by the book reviewer and critic Edmund Fuller. After earning his B. A. in English at Queens College of the City University of New York, he studied for two years at Yale Divinity School before completing his Ph.D. in American literature at Duke University. There he compiled a critical edition of Robert Frost's early poems written before 1913. A descriptive bibliography of these early unpublished and uncollected Frost poems appeared in *Proof 5*. Since then he has published other articles on Poe, Frost, Stevens, and Berryman, as well as numerous book reviews. He has also been active in drama, directing college and community theater productions. Since 1969, Angyal has taught at New Haven College, South Kent School, and Duke University, as well as serving as a public affairs officer for the U. S. Environmental Protection Agency for two years. Currently he is an assistant professor of English at Elon College in North Carolina.

Preface

Loren Eiseley remained a generalist in an age of specialists. A respected anthropologist, he preferred to write for the intelligent general reader, trusting his insights to metaphor rather than undifferentiated fact. Early in life he decided to become a writer, though he did not think he could succeed. Devoting himself instead to science, he remained a poet at heart. That poetry expressed itself through the power of his vision, spanning geological and biological time. Time in fact became the medium through which he spoke. As a scientist and poet, he wrote eloquently of man's "immense journey," blending scientific insights with moments of wonder and delight.

Eiseley was a writer of grace and eloquence both as essayist and poet, a scientist of great wisdom and insight, and an author with a wide public audience about whom little thus far has been written. Not only has his work been largely ignored by most of the literary avant-garde, he has often fallen victim to that "two cultures" split he decried in "The Illusion of the Two Cultures." Though he has done as much as anyone in his generation to revive the personal or "familiar" essay and to extend its range and audience, his contribution has gone largely unrecognized, perhaps because the literati feel less than comfortable with his subject matter and scientists too often look askance on members of their profession who write for a popular rather than a specialized audience. Yet as Van Wyck Brooks argued, our best prose is written by our natural history writers, their field dismissed by science as anachronistic and by the humanities as somehow beyond the pale.

What Eiseley's reputation will become is difficult to project so soon after his death, especially given his diverse achievements. Even if his books and essays did no more than revive public interest in the natural history essay and the accomplishments of the literary natural history writer, then, as he said in "Strangeness in the Proportion," his writing hit its mark. For Eiseley, the literary natural history writer was no Victorian anachronism, but the harbinger of a new humanism based on connections reforged between man and nature. It is clear from his final essays that his primary interest lay in the tradition of Gilbert White, W. H. Hudson, Richard

Jefferies, Ralph Waldo Emerson, Henry David Thoreau, John Muir, John Burroughs, and in our own time, writers such as Aldo Leopold, Rachel Carson, Joseph Wood Krutch, Annie Dillard, and Lewis Thomas.

Andrew J. Angyal

Elon College

Acknowledgments

This book has been made possible by the kind assistance of many individuals and institutions. I wish to express my gratitude to Mrs. Loren Eiseley for permission to quote from material under copyright with the Estate of Loren C. Eiseley. My thanks also to Francis James Dallett, University Archivist, for permission to quote from material in the University of Pennsylvania Archives, Loren Corey Eiseley Collection; and to Joseph G. Svoboda, University Archivist, for permission to quote from Eiseley's letters in the University of Nebraska–Lincoln Archives, *Prairie Schooner* editor's correspondence.

Many friends and colleagues of Loren Eiseley agreed to be interviewed or to answer my queries. I extend special thanks to them, especially Rudolph Umland, Mac Woods Bell, and Caroline Werkley.

To Elon College I am grateful for a series of summer grants that made the research for this book possible and for the sabbatical that enabled me to finish it. My thanks also to the staff of McEwen Library for their assistance and to Carolynn Lentz for typing the full manuscript through several drafts.

A number of colleagues were kind enough to read and offer their responses to various stages of the manuscript. I am particularly grateful for Professor Edwin H. Cady's editorial suggestions. And finally, my wife Jennifer spent countless hours assisting me with the editing and revisions. Without her help and support, this book would not have been possible.

For permission to quote copyrighted material from Eiseley's published works, my thanks are extended to the following publishers. To Atheneum Publishers for *The Firmament of Time,* © 1960 by Loren Eiseley, used with the permission of the publishers. To Charles Scribner's Sons for *The Night Country,* © 1971 by Loren Eiseley; *All the Strange Hours,* © 1975 by Loren Eiseley; *The Invisible Pyramid,* © 1970 by Loren Eiseley; *Notes of an Alchemist,* © 1972 by Loren Eiseley; *The Innocent Assassins,* © 1973 by Loren Eiseley; *Another Kind of Autumn,* © 1976, 1977 by the Estate of Loren Eiseley; and *The Man Who Saw Through Time,* © 1973 by Loren

Chronology

1907   Loren Corey Eiseley born, September 3, in Lincoln, Nebraska.

1913   Enters first grade in Prescott School in Lincoln.

1922–1923   Attends Lincoln High School for one year.

1923   Enters Teachers College High School of the University of Nebraska in Lincoln.

1925   June 4, graduates from Teachers College High School; September 15, enters the University of Nebraska.

1927   First poetry published in *Prairie Schooner.* Named to *Schooner* editorial staff.

1928   Drops out of university to work in poultry hatchery. March 30, father, Clyde Edwin Eiseley, dies in a Lincoln hospital. Resumes university studies.

1929   Drops out of university because of tuberculosis. Named contributing editor of *Prairie Schooner,* 1929–39. Spends summer in Colorado Rockies.

1930   Recuperates on a ranch in the Mohave Desert. Resumes university studies in the fall.

1931   Member of the South Party, Morrill Paleontological Expeditions, University of Nebraska, 1931–33.

1933   June 5, graduates from the University of Nebraska with a double major in English and sociology (concentration in anthropology). September 30, enrolls in graduate program in anthropology at University of Pennsylvania.

1934   Member of the University of Pennsylvania–Carnegie Expedition to Southwest in Search of Early Man.

1935   Completes M.A. in anthropology at University of Pennsylvania. Coauthors first professional article with Bertrand

Schultz. Returns to study in graduate school at University of Nebraska for two semesters, 1935–36.

1936 Joins the Nebraska WPA Federal Writers' Project and contributes to *Nebraska: A Guide to the Cornhusker State.*

1937 Awarded Ph.D. in anthropology from the University of Pennsylvania. Appointed assistant professor of anthropology and sociology at University of Kansas.

1938 August 29, marries Mabel Langdon in Albuquerque, New Mexico.

1940 Awarded Social Science Research Council Postdoctoral Fellowship, Columbia University and American Museum of Natural History, 1940–41.

1942 Appointed associate professor at University of Kansas. With "The Folsom Mystery," *Scientific American,* Eiseley begins writing natural history essays for popular periodicals.

1944 Appointed department chairman and professor of anthropology and sociology at Oberlin College. "The Trout," in *Prairie Schooner,* last poem to appear in print until 1964.

1947 Appointed department chairman and professor of anthropology, University of Pennsylvania, 1947–62.

1948 Named curator of early man, University of Pennsylvania Museum.

1949 President of the American Institute of Human Paleontology (until 1952).

1957 *The Immense Journey.*

1958 *Darwin's Century.*

1959 Named provost of the University of Pennsylvania, 1959–61. November 29, mother, Daisy C. Eiseley, dies in Lincoln.

1960 *The Firmament of Time.* Elected to American Philosophical Society.

1961 Named first Benjamin Franklin Professor of Anthropology and the History of Science, University of Pennsylvania.

1962   *The Mind as Nature* and *Francis Bacon and the Modern Dilemma.*

1963   Awarded a Guggenheim Fellowship, 1963–64.

1964   "Let the Red Fox Run," in *Ladies' Home Journal,* first poem to appear in twenty years.

1966   *Man, Time, and Prophecy* (private Christmas edition).

1969   *The Unexpected Universe* and *The Brown Wasps.*

1970   *The Invisible Pyramid.* June 9, delivers Harvard Phi Beta Kappa address, "Man in the Dark Wood."

1971   *The Night Country.* Elected to National Institute of Arts and Letters.

1972   *Notes of an Alchemist,* first volume of poetry.

1973   *The Innocent Assassins* (poetry), and *The Man Who Saw Through Time* (revised edition of *Francis Bacon and the Modern Dilemma*).

1974   Distinguished Nebraskan Award.

1975   *All the Strange Hours: An Excavation of a Life.*

1976   Awarded Bradford Washburn $5,000 award and gold medal for contributions to the public understanding of science.

1977   Eiseley dies of cancer in a Philadelphia hospital on July 9. *Another Kind of Autumn* (poetry).

1978   *The Star Thrower.*

1979   *Darwin and the Mysterious Mr. X: New Light on the Evolutionists* and *All the Night Wings* (poetry).

Chapter One
A Son of the "Middle Border"

In *All the Strange Hours,* Loren Eiseley describes himself as "a child of the early century." He was "a creature molded of plains' dust and the seed of those who came west with the wagons." This Great Plains sensibility runs throughout his work in descriptions of the dust and silence, the open prairies, the arid badlands, and the immense vistas of his native Nebraska. In many respects, Eiseley deserves to be ranked with Willa Cather, Mari Sandoz, John G. Niehardt, and Wright Morris as one of the outstanding authors of Great Plains literature.

Of course, Eiseley was more than another Midwestern regionalist. An eminent scientist and eloquent prose stylist, he used the Nebraska landscape as a setting for essays on the significance of geological time and organic evolution. His writing defies categories, for his interests, both scientific and literary, were far-ranging and comprehensive. In its fluent style and scientific imagination his writing resembles that of the great seventeenth-century prose stylists like Francis Bacon and Sir Thomas Browne or the nineteenth-century literary naturalists like Thoreau and W. H. Hudson. Eiseley thought of himself as a "naturalist" in the Victorian sense of a man of science with a broadly questioning mind and a gift for language. Yet he was also a poet who could balance the most abstract and speculative passages with vivid images taken from the Nebraska landscape or from his early field research.

The broad sweep of prairie landscapes Eiseley knew as a child perhaps helped him evoke reaches of geological and paleontological time that overwhelm the imagination. Few other writers have, in Bertrand Schultz's words, "been so successful in making the past live."[1] Eiseley's sense of man's insignificance in the face of geological time lends his essays and poetry a somber tone reminiscent of Ole Rölvaag's *Giants in the Earth* or Hamlin Garland's *Main-Travelled Roads,* where the prairie settlers seem transient intruders, existing at the pleasure of the climate and land. Eiseley felt great sympathy for fugitives and outcasts, for he understood

1

from childhood the struggle to survive on the small Nebraska farms and towns. When Eiseley describes himself as a son of the "middle border," he envisions that space of mid-continent "where the East was forgotten and the one great western road no longer crawled with wagons." He chose to remain a "fugitive" and a "changeling," occupying "middle borders" between science and literature, between past and present, and between fact and imagination.

Autobiographical passages in his work give poignant accounts of Eiseley's early life. His childhood was marked by isolation and loneliness, his mother's brooding possessiveness, and his sense of his family's strangeness. From earliest years he realized his difference from other children. "Terror, anxiety, ostracism, shame" were among his childhood companions. The pain of these memories is expressed in his poem "The Face of the Lion":

> I cannot practice
> the terrible archeology of the brain
> nor plumb
> one simple childhood thought.

He learned to compensate for the bleakness of this outer world by cultivating a rich inner world of his own, nourished by reading, by museum visits, and by exploring the sunflower forests of his Nebraska childhood.

Early Years

Pride in his pioneer roots and a personal obsession with the past lent Eiseley a deep interest in family genealogy. The pioneering spirit stood strongly in his grandfather, the Honorable Charles Frederick Eiseley, a German immigrant who was by turns homesteader, Indian fighter, legislator, hardware merchant, and judge. Charles's son, Clyde Edwin Eiseley, was born in 1868 on the family farm in Dodge County, Nebraska. Clyde entered his father's Norfolk hardware business and in 1892 married Anna Enderly. A son, Leo, was born two years later. Anna died of consumption in 1899, not long after the birth of a daughter, Esther, who died in infancy. Loren, the only child of his father's second marriage, remembered Clyde's inability to "bring himself to speak" of Anna, his "first love who had perished in her springtime." Her sad memory haunted his father's misbegotten second marriage to Daisy Corey in 1906.

Daisy was the child of Iowa homesteaders of English and Scottish descent. She was born in Dyerville, Iowa, in 1875. Her father, Milo, was a master carpenter who later moved with his family from Sioux City, Iowa, to Lincoln, Nebraska. Here Daisy married Clyde Eiseley, who was eight years her senior. They may have met during one of Clyde's business trips to Lincoln as a hardware salesman and been attracted to each other by common artistic interests, hers in painting and his in acting. An early photograph shows her to be an attractive woman, with dark, penetrating eyes.

Loren Corey Eiseley was born in Lincoln on September 3, 1907, ten months after Daisy and Clyde were married. As a child, Loren often wondered about this strange marriage. His mother, deafened by a childhood illness, was capable only of "negligible and disordered" speech. Her "harsh discordant jangling" voice contrasted strangely with his father's "beautiful resonant speaking voice." Clyde Eiseley had been an itinerant actor, "a largely self-trained member of one of those little troupes who played *East Lynne* and declaimed raw Shakespearean melodrama in little Midwestern 'opera houses.'" He loved language and fine rhetoric and often read aloud to his son in his rich theatrical voice, as Loren later remembered, reciting "long rolling Elizabethan passages that caused shivers to run up my back."[2]

In contrast, Loren could communicate with his deaf mother best through "hand signals, stampings on the floor to create vibrations, [and] exaggerated lip movements vaguely reminiscent of anthropoid society."[3] Her disability and isolation must have twisted her temperament, for Loren remembers her as an unstable paranoid, neurotically possessive of her son. She was a self-taught prairie artist of some talent whose ambitions, thwarted by the hardness of her life, may also have contributed to her unhappy personality. Despite his bitter memories of his mother, Loren later attributed some of his own artistic sensitivity, particularly his eidetic memory, to her.

Daisy's unstable character created conflict with her husband also. In addition, Clyde's frustrated theatrical ambitions, as well as the loss of his first wife and daughter, may have contributed to the marital tension Loren sensed even as a small child. He remembers the fear and anxiety he often felt on hearing his parents, late at night, pacing back and forth in the next room and exchanging words. Once the boy climbed out of bed and went to plead with them to stop fighting. Despite such memories, Loren recalls his father as "a good man who bore the asperities of my afflicted mother with dignity and restraint."

Those "asperities" served to isolate the entire family from the community. The Eiseleys lived in a series of small frame houses on the southern outskirts of Lincoln and kept to themselves. They moved frequently, twice to other small Nebraska towns as Clyde's fortunes as a hardware salesman fluctuated; and they had little to do with their neighbors. Their social isolation was deepened by the fact that they belonged to no church, since Daisy and Clyde could not agree on one. Loren remembered attending Sunday school only once in his life, when he was urged into an evangelical tent by his devoutly Methodist grandmother Corey.

For the most part, Loren was therefore a solitary child in an isolated family. His half-brother, Leo, fourteen years older, left home four years after Clyde's remarriage and visited only occasionally. Embarrassed by his mother's behavior, Loren was keenly aware of being "different." Once, shortly after they had moved to Aurora, Nebraska, when Loren was seeking the acceptance of a new group of children, he deliberately disobeyed Daisy's command to come home, and she ran after him into a pasture, grotesquely shouting and gesticulating. The ten-year-old boy was filled with a painful mixture of shame and guilt.

Still there was one person besides his "kind and thoughtful" father who nurtured Loren in his childhood. Daisy had a sister, Grace, who married William Buchanan "Buck" Price, a Lincoln attorney of Kentucky background. The Prices lived within a few blocks of the Eiseleys, and "Uncle Buck" took the boy on museum visits and helped him with his books and college tuition. In a copy of Henry F. Osburn's *The Origins of Evolution and Life,* which he gave to Loren on Christmas 1923, his uncle wrote "get knowledge but with it get understanding."[4] Loren was always welcome in the home of this genial, courteous man, who had no son of his own. Dedicating *All the Strange Hours,* Loren expressed appreciation to his uncle, "without whose help my life would have been different beyond imagining."

His uncle Buck and his father were Loren's two sources of stability in childhood. One of his earliest memories dated from the spring of 1910, when Loren was only three. The family had moved briefly to Fremont, Nebraska. His father took the boy outdoors in his arms one cold spring evening to watch Halley's comet mark its course through the night sky. As Eiseley recalls the incident in *The Invisible Pyramid,* his father asked him to promise that he would live long enough to witness the comet's return in 1985—a promise Loren unfortunately was not able to keep.

Books, Animals, and Museums

Loren lived in the two worlds of the exceptional child—the outer world of playmates and physical activity and the inner world of imagination. He joined other children in exploring the sunflower forests and open fields beyond the outskirts of Lincoln, and crawled through city storm sewers with his friend "Rat" until his parents put an end to that adventure. But his most poignant memories were reserved for moments of solitary play. As an only child, he must have discovered at an early age how to amuse himself with invented games, and his precocious imagination fixed upon books as soon as he learned to read. To escape from anxiety and turmoil at home, Loren turned increasingly to the worlds of books and nature to feed his inner resources and reorder his chaotic life.

Loren probably taught himself to read before kindergarten. His half-brother Leo came to visit and began reading *Robinson Crusoe* to him, but left with the book unfinished. As his autobiography describes, Loren vowed to learn how to read and discover what happened to Crusoe. Success opened the world of books for him. Once he began reading, he spent uncounted hours at the old Lincoln City Library, bringing home piles of books in a small wagon.

His parents or his aunt and uncle occasionally bought him books, especially on birthdays and at Christmas, and Loren's childhood library became so precious that he numbered and inscribed each title. He accumulated a personal library of about sixty volumes, all carefully labeled with the date and his age and address when he received them. At first he seemed to favor adventure stories like *Tom Swift* and the *Motor Boys Series,* though he soon began reading Jules Verne, Robert Louis Stevenson, and Jack London. A Victorian children's classic, Charles Kingsley's *Water Babies,* may have nourished the seeds of fantasy and wonder in his mind, insisting that nature is too strange and wonderful to be circumscribed by man: "You must not say that this cannot be, or that that is contrary to nature. You do not know what Nature is, or what she can do; and nobody knows. . . . Wise men are afraid to say there is anything contrary to nature, except what is contrary to mathematical truth . . . the wiser men are, the less they talk about 'cannot.'"[5]

Since Loren felt a great affection for animals, perhaps to compensate for the loneliness of his household and his mother's insistence that he could have no pets in the house, it is not surprising that stories such as *Black*

Beauty appeared in his library. At the age of six, he assembled a series of handwritten sketches called "Animal Aventures" [*sic*], brief stories about his uncle's dog, a kitten, a clever fox, and a mean neighborhood dog.[6] His compassion toward animals is particularly evident in the last sketch, "Animal Kindness," where he describes how he gradually befriended a large dog that barked every day on his way to school. His accounts of rescuing a stunned woodpecker and putting gold-painted crosses in a small animal graveyard in a vacant lot across from his home also date from this period.

In a tenth-grade essay assignment, Loren expressed his desire to become a nature writer, no doubt inspired by his reading of Ernest Thompson Seton and perhaps Henri Fabre. He still cherished animals, judging from another essay entitled "Whiskers" about a pet killed by a neighboring farmer's dogs. His reaction demonstrates his willingness to view all animals as fellow creatures: "I remembered what the big folks said about heaven and was content until I learned that church people didn't seem to think animals went to heaven. I was terribly hurt at this and I don't believe I've ever had as good an opinion of God's judgment since."[7]

Loren also loved natural history books. Eugene Smith's *The Home Aquarium: How to Care for It* taught him how to build his own aquarium and stock it with fresh-water fish and invertebrates from local ponds and streams. After reading Smith's book, Loren was inspired to make a homemade aquarium from wood, glass, and tar, and march off to a frozen pond to chop through the ice and dredge for specimens. From Smith's book, he also learned simple lessons in ecology.

During his childhood in Lincoln, Eiseley frequented the museum at the University of Nebraska. His uncle Buck first took him to the old red-brick building containing mammoth bones and other paleontological exhibits from the Nebraska Badlands and elsewhere in the state. In *The Night Country* he describes his fascination with the skulls in the museum. Later, at home, he would shape small clay skulls and bake them in the oven, much to the consternation of his pious Methodist grandmother. Afterward he would take them up to the loft of a nearby stable and place them in rows along the cross-beams, creating a miniature anthropological museum for himself. Whether or not this story is apocryphal, it still reflects Loren's early curiosity about human evolution and the origins of man.

Aside from a brief period when his family lived in Fremont from 1909 to 1911 and another move to Aurora in 1917–18, Loren spent most of his childhood at four Lincoln addresses. He attended elementary grades at Prescott School until 1922, then entered Lincoln High School for one year to complete his tenth grade. At Lincoln High he was so timid that when a teacher invited him to join the debating club, he was too terrified to accept.[8] Because of adjustment problems he dropped out of high school briefly, but returned to complete his junior and senior years at Temple or University Teachers College High School, a highly reputed school run by the University of Nebraska Education Department.

At Temple High Loren played football and was involved in dramatics while still completing a college preparatory program with respectable grades. An English teacher there, Miss Letta Clark, recognized his talent for writing and encouraged him to continue. About this time he began writing free verse for his own pleasure, though he probably did not show it to anyone and none of it has survived. Compared to his childhood, Loren mentioned little about his teenage years. An incident from his junior year, however, marked his discovery of time's arrow. One day, while leaning from a classroom window, he noticed a junkman and his cart passing the intersection between R and Fourteenth streets, a block away. This sudden glimpse filled Loren with a deep nostalgia for the passing and unrecoverable moment. He vowed to fix the scene in his mind and "immortalize" it there. This obsession with time's elusiveness later became a predominant theme in his work. Otherwise Eiseley is silent about these years, though records show that he performed well enough at Teachers College High School to earn his diploma in June, 1925, and enter the University of Nebraska as a freshman that fall.

College Years

Loren entered the College of Arts and Sciences at the University of Nebraska in September, 1925, although he would not complete his undergraduate degree for another eight years. His restless, unsettled temperament and a series of personal calamities intervened to postpone his graduation until the spring of 1933. Even before his father's death in March, 1928, Eiseley had dropped out of school for one semester; this was probably when he began "bumming about" the West on freight trains. Financial pressures, illness, or personal problems also interrupted his studies in other semesters.

Friends from this period remember him as a serious student, often aloof and preoccupied. Somewhat shy and awkward in company, he once climbed atop a windmill at a party to get away from the crowd. Preston Holder, a fellow student and poet, remembers Loren as "a morose romantic and somehow doomed figure from some 19th century Russian novel."[9] Another friend, Rudolph Umland, writes about these years:

[Professor Lowry] Wimberly said he used to see Loren walking across the campus with a bleak look on his face as if he had just been kicked off a freight train. Loren never outgrew his feeling of isolation but came to recognize it in himself and shielded it so carefully that it often passed unnoticed.[10]

That these were years of great personal pain and difficulty is evident from the autobiography. Clyde Eiseley moved from Lincoln back to Norfolk in November, 1927, to wQrk for a hardware firm in that city and hoped eventually to relocate his family there. This separation from his father began a traumatic series of events for Loren. Within six months, his father died of stomach cancer at the age of sixty. His belief in Christian Science may have dissuaded him from seeking medical attention until it was too late. Loren witnessed his father's suffering during the final weeks of his illness, and the shock of his death brought him close to a nervous breakdown. In *The Night Country,* Eiseley describes how his fear and grief brought about an insomnia that was to trouble him for the rest of his life.[11] Fortunately his grandmother Corey recognized his problem and came to comfort him during his sleepless nights.

His father's death also left Loren and his mother so impoverished they were forced to move in with his uncle Buck Price and his family. Since they were now without an income, Loren's mother may have urged him to drop out of college and find work to support them. His uncle generously offered money for books and tuition, but Loren was forced to begin working nights in a local chicken hatchery in order to continue his studies. In *All the Strange Hours,* Eiseley recalls the strain of this work, which required him to awaken every hour and check the kerosene incubators because of the potential fire hazard.

After several months of this, Loren's health had deteriorated so much that he went to the university dispensary, where a doctor discovered incipient tuberculosis. The physician callously remarked within Loren's hearing that he doubted the boy had many months to live. Eiseley was forced to withdraw from college for three semesters until his health improved. His aunt Price agreed to spend the summer with him in the higher altitudes of the Colorado Rockies, but nevertheless, when he was reexamined that fall, the doctor told him that he needed additional rest. Through the generosity of a professor at the university, Loren arranged to take a leave of absence during the 1929–30 academic year and recuperate on a turkey ranch in the Mohave Desert of California, where he served as a caretaker in the company of an amiable ex-convict, Nelson Goodfellow.

A year later, largely recovered, Eiseley drifted back East on the freight trains in the company of other homeless and jobless men. He resumed his university studies in the fall of 1930, this time determined to graduate. Perhaps more than anything else his interest in poetry drew Loren back to Lincoln, the scene of so much that was painful during these years.

As an undergraduate Loren was a gifted student, but shy and sensitive to criticism. His father had written before his death that "the boy is a genius, but moody." A fellow student later remembered Eiseley as "a rather strange fellow, a loner, who was very much interested in writing during this time." In Professor Kenneth Forward's course in the nineteenth-century essay, the students were assigned to write a theme on an essayist of their choice for the final exam.[12] While other students dutifully completed the assignment, Loren stared at the paper with distaste, and finally wrote a poem instead. At the end of the exam he submitted the poem rather than the required essay. After two days of indecision, Forward gave Eiseley an "A" in the course, thus assuring his continued friendship with this brilliant but unconventional student.

Eiseley showed the same creativity and originality in other essay assignments. For one theme in Forward's class Loren had written a personal essay describing three of his homes in Lincoln and the unnatural atmosphere his mother's deafness had brought to each. Later, during one of their walks, Eiseley pointed out each of these houses to his professor. Forward was so impressed with the evocative power of Loren's essay that he retraced the same route with another student five or six years later.[13] Another prose sketch that probably originated as a class assignment, "Autumn—A Memory," later appeared in the October, 1927, issue of the *Prairie Schooner*.[14] This brief sketch evokes an autumnal mood of sadness and loss through the narrator's reflections on the fate of the people who once inhabited the Aztec ruins. One line in particular—"I was a shadow among shadows brooding over the fate of other shadows that I alone strove to summon up out of the all-pervading dusk"—hints at Eiseley's promise as a master of lyrical prose. After pausing to notice signs of former habitation, Loren reflects on what caused the decline of this once flourishing culture. The theme of extinction—personal and collective—that would become so important in his later works is introduced here for the first time.

Outside of class, much of Eiseley's time was devoted to campus literary affairs. In 1932, he joined the local chapter of Sigma Epsilon, a national literary fraternity. With the support of Lowry C. Wimberly of the English Department, the Wordsworth Chapter in Lincoln had been instrumental in founding the University of Nebraska literary magazine, the *Prairie Schooner*. Loren may have met his future wife, Mabel Langdon, through these activities, and he was introduced to Professor Wimberly, who became Eiseley's friend and literary mentor. Loren became a member of the

Wimberly circle of early *Schooner* contributors and was soon named to the editorial staff, first as a poetry editor and later as a contributing editor from 1929 to 1939.

Wimberly had recently published his *Folklore in the English and Scottish Ballads* and was known in Lincoln as something of a literary iconoclast for his sharp satires of several university administrators. Determined to promote Midwest regional writing, he fought deans and chancellors to keep his magazine funded when its subsidy was threatened. Through the *Schooner* Wimberly encouraged talent and creativity among his students and followers, and became an important influence in shaping the literary aspirations of both Mari Sandoz and Loren Eiseley, who both first published there while each was an undergraduate.[15]

Despite his avid interest in poetry and the *Prairie Schooner,* the trauma of these years played upon Eiseley's imagination and left him permanently a fugitive, outcast from the normal world. Later he could be stoical and reserved, compassionate and even gravely humorous, but never happy. He had been too deeply scarred by these early experiences ever to forget. Eventually they would be reshaped as the most moving passages in *The Night Country* and *All the Strange Hours.* Edgar Allan Poe's "Alone" became the poem of Eiseley's extended adolescence; he tacked it above the bench at which he worked part-time at the University Museum, and when someone passing read the poem and cracked a joke, he was deeply offended.

If love for poetry brought Loren back to Lincoln, he soon realized that it would not earn him a living. In desperation he looked for alternatives. While he had concentrated on English and philosophy during his first few years of college, he now turned to anthropology, a young science still offered by the Sociology Department. He took two anthropology courses that opened new prospects to his imagination—natural history might serve as a metaphor for personal history—a "natural history" of the mind.

The fall of 1930 found Eiseley back in Lincoln at the age of twenty-five with scarcely enough credits to rank as a junior after five years of intermittent study. The romance of hoboing and the desire to complete college pulled him in opposite directions, but the economic hardships evident everywhere gave his studies new urgency. He saw that he would have to finish his education soon if he was to finish at all. To continue aimless wandering would be to court oblivion. Chapter 7 of his autobiography, "The Most Perfect Day in the World," indicates how strong a hold self-destructive impulses had upon his imagination.

That fall, Eiseley met a Nebraska undergraduate from Red Cloud, Bertrand Schultz, who later became an eminent vertebrate paleontologist.

The two, who formed a lifelong friendship, discovered a shared interest in geological history and the question of the antiquity of man in North America.[16] That semester both became field assistants in William Duncan Strong's course, "Field and Museum Techniques in Anthropology." Their professor thought so well of Schultz and Eiseley that he often let them supervise weekend digs along the Missouri Bluffs near Omaha. Loren later said that Dr. Strong "lured me into Anthropology as a major subject."

The South Party

By the following spring, Eiseley decided that he was tired of archeological digs. He wanted more experience in paleontology. Dr. Erwin H. Barbour, the new director of the Morrill Museum, knew about Loren's writing ability and his interest in natural history, and found funds to permit Eiseley to join the Museum's South Party that summer. For the next three seasons, Loren would go on the South Party's summer field expeditions to western Nebraska. Every member of the party kept a field notebook to record the finds and sites of important specimens, and Loren's notebooks later became a rich source of images and anecdotes for his writing.

The South Party had been organized by Dr. Barbour, who was interested in sending collecting parties to the Badlands region during this early period in American paleontology, when the rich fossil fields of Nebraska, South Dakota, Wyoming, and Colorado were still being explored. Important fossil discoveries had recently been made and major museums were eager to obtain specimens of extinct North American mammals. Though Eiseley and Schultz briefly considered becoming professional bone hunters, after several years of summer field work Loren's allergies to dust and pollen caused him to change his plans.

Eiseley first joined the South Party in the summer of 1931, when some of its members made important paleontological discoveries on Wildcat Ridge in western Nebraska's Banner County, an area of rugged pine-covered hills that stretch into Wyoming. During most of the summer their finds were scanty—"one Oligocene turtle and a bag of rhinoceros bones"—but late in the season they got word from an old rancher of a potential fossil quarry on the Emerson Fayden Ranch. The rancher, an amateur bone hunter, took them to a site on Wildcat Mountain where the bones of shovel-tusked mastodons and bearlike dogs were eroding out of the sediment. A fictionalized account of this discovery later appeared in "The Relic Men," chapter 8 of *The Night Country.*

The following spring Dr. Barbour had Schultz and Eiseley rearrange their academic schedules so he could send them into the field six weeks early to begin work at the Emerson Fayden Ranch. Barbour was anxious to collect enough mastodon bones to add a skeleton or two to the newly completed elephant hall of the Morrill Museum. Later in the spring of 1932, the party learned of a site west of Scottsbluff where hundreds of exposed bones had been discovered in a stream bank. The site appeared promising, so they set up camp there and opened the now famous Scottsbluff Bison Quarry. In August of that year, eight artifacts of early man were found associated with the bones of extinct bison. As Bertrand Schultz later remarked, "a new chapter in American archeology had been written." A new cultural complex had been discovered, dating back almost 10,000 years, which strongly suggested that man had inhabited North America much earlier than was previously thought. This discovery led to Eiseley's first professional article, coauthored with Bertrand Schultz in the *American Anthropologist,* in which they tried to convince skeptics that early man did occupy North America long before 2,000 years ago.[17]

After two seasons with the South Party, Eiseley had shown academic credentials and field experience so good that Dr. Barbour hired him part-time at the University Museum, where he cleaned, polished, and assembled bones. Barbour also urged him to apply for graduate work in anthropology at the University of Pennsylvania. By the time he entered, in the fall of 1933, Loren had acquired wide practical experience in geology, archeology, and paleontology to balance his academic training at the University of Nebraska. More immediately, his field work was a source of badly needed income, for he had virtually supported himself since his father's death.

In the summer of 1933, Eiseley worked for the South Party one final season. A highlight of that summer was the discovery of the remains of a twenty-million-year-old Miocene cat, whose sabers had penetrated the scapula of another cat. Both animals had probably starved to death or died of injuries, unable to escape. This skull, with its saber still embedded in a fossilized scapula bone, remains on display in the Morrill Museum.

Once Eiseley began graduate study, he returned to the field for two seasons: with the University of Pennsylvania–Carnegie Expedition to the Southwest in Search of Early Man in 1934, and with the Smithsonian Expedition to northern Colorado in 1935. After that year, the demands of graduate work prevented him from joining summer field parties until he had completed his doctorate in 1937.

During these summers of apprentice training in paleontology, Eiseley neither entirely gave up his interest in poetry nor lost his restlessness. On weekends or in the evenings at camp he wrote letters to friends in Lincoln about submissions to the *Prairie Schooner* or poems in progress. His romantic spirit expressed itself in this May 20, 1932, letter to Wilbur Gaffney from a camp near Redington, Nebraska:

Here where there are only bones asleep in their million-year old rotting, where the events of the Pliocene seem more real than those of civilization—that overnight fungus, you may take it as a compliment that I was genuinely moved by these sonnets. Love is a faint far cry along the wind here—an old troubling lament from the world's edge that came to me in your letter. Not real. Something suffered a long time ago before I stepped out of time. That is the way it is here. Or was. Yesterday a pretty young gypsy waved at me from a camp by the road. It took me a whole day to forget—not very successfully. Why? I don't know—except that she was beautiful—and I was young—and we would never see each other again and never speak. And she was one of the outcast people among whom I should have been born—the people who have no ties but a duty to horizons, who never grow old as we do squatting by the little fire of memory that goes out and leaves us to freeze alone in the end. . . . Tell me again the name of that book in which a man escaped his world by way of a pedlar's cart. I must read something of that before I find myself taking root and turning into a yucca plant on one of these bare hillsides. . . .[18]

Many of Eiseley's permanent themes emerge in this remarkable letter—his sense of man's transience, his wariness about love, his desire somehow to "escape" the burden of time, and again, of course, his temperamental gloom, his sense of himself as an "outcast." The book about the man who "escaped from his world by way of a pedlar's cart" was W. J. Locke's *The Golden Journey of Mr. Paradyne,* a romantic novel about Gypsies that apparently fascinated Eiseley, since he several times used that image in his mature writings. *The Night Country,* for instance, begins with a description in "The Golden Wheel" of the incident during Loren's childhood when he tried to run away on the back of a brightly colored tea wagon.

Sometimes on weekends during these field expeditions Eiseley would seek out the hoboes camped at a local railroad siding and swap stories with them about dodging "railroad bulls" and riding long freights over the Western plains. These experiences from his period of drifting after he withdrew from college found their way into two of his early short stories,

"Riding the Peddlers" and "The Mop to K.C.," both published during
the 1930s in the *Prairie Schooner.* "The Mop to K.C." was even mentioned
on the honor roll of *O'Brien's Best Short Stories of 1936.*[19] Along with many
of his college friends, Eiseley found the urge to ride the rails particularly
strong during the depression years, when jobs were scarce and extra
mouths to feed were a burden at home. Part of the fascination of hoboing
was the romance and adventure of wandering through the West living the
life of a vagabond, although Eiseley also mentions in *All the Strange Hours*
how dangerous all that could be. He describes how he nearly lost his life
one night while riding behind the coal tender of a fast passenger train,
when, through fatigue, he almost lost his grip and fell under the wheels.
Nevertheless, Loren continued to ride the rails whenever he could.

Eiseley later drew heavily on his South Party field experiences as a source
of literary inspiration, even dedicating his second book of poetry, *The
Innocent Assassins,* "to the bone hunters of the old South Party." The field
notebooks, with their notations about fossil finds and Badlands stratigraphy, inspired many a poem or essay. Often Eiseley began with the kernel
of an actual field happening and selectively altered or fictionalized it to
heighten a mood or tone, or else to emphasize some theme or motif. In
such writing, as the incident unfolds natural history gradually becomes a
metaphor for personal history as the author probes the recesses in his mind.

The summer field work at Scottsbluff in 1932, culminating in the
discovery of human artifacts with the bones of extinct bison, first led
Schultz and Eiseley to publish their findings in 1935 and then to plan a
book for Macmillan entitled "They Hunted the Mammoth," the story of
early man in North America. Several initial chapters had even been
approved for publication when the outbreak of World War II made the
completion of the project inopportune. Loren's contributions to this book,
which was never completed, later appeared in a series of professional and
popular essays during the 1940s, and their reception may have encouraged
his development as a personal essayist.[20]

The discovery of the bone quarry on the Emerson Fayden Ranch in the
summer of 1931 appears in chapter 8 of *The Night Country.* The contrast
between the account described in "The Relic Men" and the recollections of
other members of the South Party provides useful hints about Eiseley's
methods of composition.[21] As he dramatizes his first impressions of the
site:

I saw the ivory from tusks of elephants scattered like broken china that the
rain has washed. I saw the splintered, mineralized enamel of huge, unknown

teeth. I paused over the bones of ferocious bear-dog carnivores. I saw, protruding from an eroding gully, the jaw of a shovel-tusked amebelodont that has been gone twice a million years into the night of geologic time. I tell you I saw it with my own eyes and I knew, even as I looked at it, that I would never see anything like it again. (122)

What Eiseley did in this account was to rearrange and edit "experience" into an evocative sketch—something approaching the short story. He used fictional devices to establish conflict and suspense and to add unity and a focus that his first record lacked. In short, he now tells the story with a novelist's eye, as it should happen for the reader, not necessarily as it first struck him. Though most descriptive details stay unaltered and the narrative keeps an authentic Western flavor, the events may not have taken place in the same sequence or with the particular characters he mentions. The old fundamentalist Mullens and his family perhaps appear when and where they do because they make a good story. Does it matter whether it was at first on their ranch where the fossil quarry was actually found? There were in fact many such farm families in the dry, marginal lands of western Nebraska, hostile and suspicious toward the notion of evolution, accounting for the bones on their land in terms of Noah's Flood.

An encounter with a pair of nesting sparrow hawks at a field site in the spring of 1932 formed the germ of another incident Eiseley described in *The Immense Journey*. Before members of the South Party could move into an abandoned stone cabin, Eiseley had to clean it out and make it fit for human habitation. The sparrow hawks had made their nest among the eaves, and Loren had to find a way to evict them. The female left immediately, but it was not until the next morning that they could get the male to leave also. He kept darting in and out among the eaves.

Once again Eiseley took an experience from his South Party days and heightened and intensified it by selectively altering the context and dramatizing the situation. In his essay "The Bird and the Machine" the members of the field party were trapping and collecting birds to restock a zoo. Loren describes himself as a "skilled assassin," capturing birds at their roosts. The struggle with the nesting pair is dramatically strengthened, with the male altruistically saving his mate through a diversion by attacking Eiseley with his beak and claws. After he was finally captured, the male sparrow hawk was caged until the next morning, when, in a moment of compassion, Loren impulsively decided to release him. The reunion of the two hawks circling high in the firmament became one of the most beautifully realized moments in Eiseley's writing:

I saw them both now. He was rising fast to meet her. They met in a great soaring gyre that turned to a whirling circle and a dance of wings. Once more, just once, their two voices, joined in a harsh wild medley of question and response, struck and echoed against the pinnacles of the valley. Then they were gone forever somewhere into those upper regions beyond the eyes of men. (192)

The drama of the male sparrow hawk's capture and caging makes the moment of his release and reunion with his mate climactic to the essay, in contrast with the machine, which "does not bleed, ache, hang for hours in the empty sky in a torment of hope to learn the fate of another machine, nor does it cry out with joy nor dance in the air with the fierce passion of a bird."

The discovery of the sabertooth skull that excited Eiseley's imagination during the summer of 1933 would find its way into the title poem of his second volume of poetry. In "The Innocent Assassins," Loren imaginatively re-created the sequence of events suggested by the unusual fossil find forty million years later. The literary work both marvels at these perfected, though long extinct, instruments of death and weeps for man, "who knows this antique trade / but is not guiltless."

Eiseley's childhood and his days with the South Party became a well of experience upon which he drew for much of his later work. More than any others, these were the events that fixed themselves in his memory to be transmuted by his imagination into the compact and powerful metaphoric descriptions that distinguish his style.

Frank Speck: The Last Shaman

When Eiseley arrived in Philadelphia in the fall of 1933 to begin his graduate study of anthropology at the University of Pennsylvania, he entered a department with only three full-time faculty members. Eleven other students enrolled that fall, not all of whom could attend full-time. Sunburned and toughened by the hard labor of digging fossils for the South Party, Loren impressed his fellow graduate students with the wealth of his field experience in geology and paleontology. Yet, coming straight from the Nebraska Badlands, Loren found the noise and congestion of Philadelphia almost unendurable, and it took him several days to adjust. Eventually, however, he found haven, perhaps appropriately, in the University's International House.

Eiseley soon became acquainted with the departmental chairman, Dr. Frank G. Speck, a noted ethnologist and expert on the Eastern Woodland

Indians, who was to become Loren's dissertation director and close personal friend. Speck was something of a maverick academician—a short, broad-shouldered man with the build of a New England sea captain, who preferred strenuous field work to the formalities of academe. A noted scholar, Speck was an authority on Indian customs and traditions, a pioneer in ethnohistory, and one of the last of the "old school" of field anthropologists who worked directly with the disappearing remnants of the Mohegan, Seneca, and Algonkian cultures. He had studied anthropology at Columbia University under Franz Boas, the department that had also produced Ralph Linton, Margaret Mead, Ruth Benedict, and many another. An excellent linguist with an almost uncanny ability to transliterate and record Native American speech, Speck could enter into the mindsets of cultures he studied. Often he brought Indians to class, conversed with them in their own language, and required his graduate students to make phonetic notations of their speech. His intense interest in American Indians may have stemmed from a period in his childhood when he was cared for by an elderly Connecticut Mohegan woman. He recognized the importance of collecting information about the material culture, social institutions, and folklore of the Eastern Woodlands tribes while they were still extant. Speck was an active scholar and a fluent stylist who saw the value of continually publishing professional papers and urged his students to do the same. Eiseley may well have been influenced by Speck's graceful personal style and by his vividly imaginative essays on ethnology, which read more like literary essays than professional articles.

At that time, anthropology students were expected to make frequent visits to the zoological gardens to observe primates. Speck required his students to identify the various species at sight, and at least one of Eiseley's poems, "Incident at the Zoo," was probably written after a visit with Speck to the Philadelphia Zoo. Interest in natural history was closely related to Speck's work in ethnology, and he retained a lifelong interest in birds, snakes, and plants, even publishing a number of articles in various fields of natural history. One of the ways he might test the mettle of a new graduate student would be slowly to draw a snake from a bag and place it on his desk without batting an eye. If the student held his ground and did not display fear, he generally won Speck's approval. Despite such eccentricities Speck was an informal and genial professor who encouraged students to visit his office after class and continue their discussions over coffee around his large desk. Often these groups would adjourn to a restaurant on Woodland Avenue, where the professor would bet against any student taker on the number of the next trolley car to go by. At the end of their first semester, Eiseley's class felt comfortable enough with Speck to buy him a box of cigars.

In Loren's first semester of classes, Speck had shown his ethnology class a small heap of square-cut flints and asked them to identify the pieces. When Loren correctly identified them as eighteenth-century gun flints, he immediately won his professor's regard. Speck gradually came to serve both as a professional role model and something of a father-figure to provide the stabilizing influence Loren had lacked since his own father's death five years earlier.

Eiseley's intellectual debt to Frank Speck was considerable. What Loren particularly gained from him was an appreciation of the poetic qualities of the Indian mind as revealed in its animistic beliefs and an understanding of the function of the Indian shaman as a visionary medium between man and animal. The poetic implications of these Native American beliefs, particularly the imagery of the animal totem figures, obviously caught Eiseley's imagination. Many of his later poems, particularly in his first three volumes of poetry, concentrate either on imaginative extensions of the human consciousness into the animal or on mystical encounters between man and animal that suggest a "poetic shamanism." The shamanistic perspective enabled him to convey in metaphoric terms his consciousness of evolutionary change through a series of visionary extensions backward through time and outward from man to his fellow creatures. Such an animism also allowed him to express his deep compassion for kindred forms of life without appearing sentimental. Furthermore, the use of ethnological folklore and primitive religious beliefs in his poems encouraged Eiseley to move beyond the derivative poetry of undergraduate years and gradually to discover his own poetic voice.

Eiseley's graduate study with Frank Speck eventually grew into close friendship between these two men of different generations who both perceived themselves to be unconventional anthropologists. Speck on his part was sufficiently impressed with his grave and serious graduate student from Nebraska to invite him on occasional weekend canoeing trips on the Delaware River or hiking excursions into the New Jersey Pine Barrens. Later they collaborated on two studies dealing with the hunting territory systems of the Algonkian.[22] Ten years after he was awarded his doctorate, Eiseley returned to the University of Pennsylvania and in 1947 succeeded his former dissertation advisor as chairman of the Anthropology Department.

In the summer of 1934 Eiseley joined the University of Pennsylvania– Carnegie Expedition to the Southwest in Search of Early Man. The following summer he was a member of the Smithsonian Expedition to Northern Colorado led by his former Nebraska professor, Dr. William D. Strong. The expedition worked the famous Lindenmeier site near Fort Collins. During these two seasons he was actively involved in the search for early postglacial man in North America, a quest which took him back to the high plains, mountains, and deserts of the West. These expeditions inspired several of Eiseley's later works, including the early sketch "Underground," and three articles published in *Harper's* between 1947 and 1951, "Obituary of a Bone Hunter," "Buzby's Petrified Woman," and "People Leave Skulls With Me," which were subsequently revised and appeared as chapters in *The Night Country*.[23]

Loren did well enough during his first year of graduate study at Pennsylvania to be awarded a Harrison Scholarship the following year. After two years at Pennsylvania he earned a master's degree in 1935, presenting "A Summary of the Paleontological Evidence Bearing on the Antiquity of the Scottsbluff Quarry" for his thesis. It was an early draft of the article Schultz and Eiseley were to publish in the *American Anthropologist* that same year.[24]

The Nebraska Federal Writers' Project

Eiseley's graduate studies at Pennsylvania were interrupted in 1935 by financial constraints caused in part by the sudden death of his uncle, on August 19, which forced him to return to Lincoln and look after his mother and aunt. Having completed most of the course work for his doctorate, he felt he could study to pass his foreign language requirement more cheaply at home. During the 1935–36 academic year Loren reentered the University of Nebraska and took three sociology courses each semester and a German reading course for graduate students. While in Lincoln he hoped to support himself with a librarian's position at the Morrill Museum, but the appointment did not materialize. By the end of the winter, short of money and desperate for work, Loren spoke with Professor Wimberly, who urged him to apply at the Nebraska Federal Writers' Project.

In February, 1936, Eiseley started work on the Writers' Project in Lincoln where Rudolph Umland, then state editor, assigned him to research and write essays on geology, paleontology, and prehistoric Indian culture for the state guidebook.[25] These sections of the *Nebraska* guide reveal Eiseley's detailed knowledge of the natural history of his state and the firsthand experience he had gained from his field work, but they show little of his distinctive style. Their dry, expository approach probably reflects at least some editorial revision to maintain the guide's unity and consistency. At least the section on prehistoric Indian culture allowed him to discuss some of the Scottsbluff artifacts, perhaps dating back 10,000 to 12,000 years, which Eiseley and Schultz had recently announced in the *American Anthropologist*.

Eiseley's brief tenure with the Nebraska Writers' Project enabled him to renew acquaintance with other members of the *Prairie Schooner* staff who were now on the WPA payroll. For a few months, at least, he was back in the company of writers and poets, some of whom he had known during his undergraduate years. Research for the state guide also put Loren back in touch with his roots. In a moment of shared confidence he pointed to a map of Nebraska and showed state editor Umland the Dodge County location where his grandfather had homesteaded. His assignments as a staff writer gave him practice in casting scientific expertise in the form of the popular essay, a genre to which he would increasingly turn during the next ten years. He was even mentioned briefly in the *Nebraska* guide as a young state poet of promise, who had contributed "poems of individuality and power" to the *Prairie Schooner* and other little magazines.[26]

Graduation and Marriage

After a few months with the Nebraska Writers' Project, Eiseley left the position to study for his foreign language examination, which he passed that summer. Then, after joining his future wife and her family for a brief vacation in Colorado and visiting Bert Schultz's field site in western Nebraska, Loren returned to the University of Pennsylvania, where a Harrison Fellowship eased his financial situation during the 1936–37 academic year. During his year in Lincoln he had been preparing a second professional article with Bert Schultz, "An Added Note on the Scottsbluff Quarry," which was published in the *American Anthropologist* in the summer of 1936. This additional information on the Folsom and Yuma artifacts led directly to his doctoral dissertation proposal.

Inspired by his recent field work and the published articles on the Scottsbluff discoveries, Eiseley decided to investigate the usefulness of various scientific measurements of Quaternary time in the study of early man. His dissertation title became "Three Indices of Quaternary Time and Their Bearing on the Problem of American Prehistory: A Critique."[27] There he examined the scientific literature on Quaternary chronology in an attempt to relate invertebrate and vertebrate successions as they influenced the determination of glacial and postglacial time in North America. In addition, he included a critique of pollen analysis as a method of dating archeological artifacts. One of the chapters of his dissertation, "Index Mollusca and Their Bearing on Certain Problems of Prehistory: A Critique," was published as part of the *Twenty-Fifth Anniversary Series of the Philadelphia Anthropological Society.*[28]

Through his work with the Folsom and Yuma artifacts and his dissertation research, Eiseley was increasing his command of physical anthropology and paleoarcheology. His interest in these fields gave him a special appreciation of how early man had adapted to climatic and other environmental changes during the last glacial period. Man was shaped and hardened by the rigors of survival in a world of flora and fauna ever retreating before the apparently endless advance of winter. When Eiseley began, many anthropologists believed that the human brain had suddenly and dramatically increased in size during the recent interglacial periods, though this assumption has since been called into question by the discovery of more ancient hominoid remains in the Olduvai Gorge and elsewhere. For Eiseley, *Homo sapiens* was in a particular sense a creature of ice and snow, and from glacial landscapes he chose the metaphors which most often expressed his imaginative sense of man as a survivor of the great Pleistocene extinctions.

In June, 1937, Eiseley was awarded his doctorate in anthropology from the University of Pennsylvania. He stood alone to receive his degree, with no friends or family members present at the ceremony. A completed dissertation did not guarantee anyone a teaching position in 1937, however. That summer Loren despaired of finding an academic appointment and even briefly considered becoming a journalist until the University of Kansas offered him an assistant professorship in anthropology and sociology. His first year of teaching at Kansas may have been a somewhat traumatic experience for him. He later bemusedly compared his first efforts before an introductory sociology class to "the proverbial Russian fleeing in a sleigh across the steppes before a wolf pack," desperately throwing scraps of information to his pursuers. Somehow he survived the year, however, with the respect of his chairman, Professor Carroll Clark.

Secure in his appointment, Eiseley married Mabel Langdon, on August 29, 1938, in Albuquerque, New Mexico, a year after he received his doctorate. They had met in 1925, as undergraduates at the University of Nebraska, when Loren was a freshman and Mabel was a senior, though both were English majors with an interest in poetry. Mabel was also a member of the "Wimberly Circle" and eventually contributed to the

Prairie Schooner, writing poetry and literary reviews. As their acquaintance grew Loren and Mabel often went for long walks in the rolling hills and farmland surrounding Lincoln, where they would picnic and read poetry aloud to each other—selections such as MacLeish's epic poem *Conquistador.* In one of their undergraduate courses, Mabel humorously chided Loren for composing poetry in his notebook during the professor's lecture. Beside Loren's poem she wrote, "Remember, this is a history course."

They continued to see each other during the 1930s and Mabel visited Loren several times in Philadelphia, but financial constraints made marriage impossible. After Mabel's graduation from Nebraska in 1925, where she had majored in English and studied French and fine arts, she may have looked briefly for a teaching position before she returned to Lincoln as a graduate student in English for two more years, from 1926 to 1928. Then she went to work for Professor Dwight Kirsch, director of the School of Fine Arts. Mabel was soon promoted to assistant curator, and by 1931 she had become a curator of the Nebraska fine arts collection, then housed in the Morrill Museum. After her marriage to Loren, Mabel continued her interest in fine arts administration and eventually became assistant director of the distinguished Pennsylvania Academy of Fine Arts in Philadelphia.

Despite the pressures of two careers, the Eiseleys enjoyed a supportive marriage between professional people who took an active interest in each other's work. Part of their honeymoon was spent at one of Loren's field sites, "poking into caves and looking at all kinds of 'fascinating' archeological remains," as Mabel later remarked in a letter to a friend. Even before they were married, Mabel typed many of Loren's papers, and she continued to assist him with the editing and preparation of his manuscripts, since Loren primarily composed his drafts by hand. Throughout their marriage, Mabel provided the security, order, and stability Loren required, and he felt disoriented when she went away on an occasional trip. An extremely private person, Mabel Eiseley chose not to take part in her husband's public life, particularly after Loren became an established writer in the 1960s. Largely through her urging, Eiseley refrained from mentioning her in his autobiography and concentrated instead on his childhood and early years. They had no children, partly for medical reasons, and partly because of Loren's fear of passing on his mother's instability.

On the Trail of Folsom Man

Eiseley found a congenial academic environment at the University of Kansas, largely because his department chairman, Carroll D. Clark, encouraged Loren's research interests. Continuing his search for evidence of early man's presence on the Great Plains, Eiseley spent several summers investigating Smith and Doniphan County field sites in western and northeastern Kansas. After three years of teaching he was awarded a postdoctoral fellowship to study ethnology and physical anthropology for a year at Columbia University and the American Museum of Natural History. When he returned to Kansas, he was promoted to associate professor.

With the advent of World War II, Eiseley volunteered for service but was rejected because of his poor eyesight and hearing and because he was the sole support of his widowed mother and aunt. He had briefly hoped to obtain a military staff position on one of the Pacific islands. Instead, the remainder of the war years found him devoting most of his time to teaching anatomy at the University of Kansas Medical School because of the urgent need for doctors and the shortage of medical faculty. The chairman of the Anatomy Department, Dr. H. C. Tracy, was so impressed with Loren's abilities that he offered personally to arrange his admission to medical school. Though honored by the gesture, Eiseley felt that at the age of thirty-seven he was too old to enter a new profession. Neither could he afford to return to school, with his mother and aunt to support.

Another academic offer came in the spring of 1944. He was offered the chairmanship of the Department of Sociology and Anthropology at Oberlin College. The research opportunities were better there than at Kansas, so in August, 1944, Eiseley resigned his position to accept the Oberlin appointment that September. With the move, Loren was also promoted to full professor. At Oberlin he actively built library holdings, but raised comments by teaching in a turtleneck sweater.

Eiseley remained at Oberlin College for three years before being invited to become chairman of the Anthropology Department at the University of Pennsylvania. Eager to return to Philadelphia, he immediately accepted the appointment. It meant rebuilding the Anthropology Department at Pennsylvania, languishing after the loss of Frank Speck. Carl Wittke, the dean of faculty at Oberlin, was reluctant to lose a popular professor, but he wrote Loren a warm recommendation for his new position. About this time, Eiseley was forced to give up a projected research trip to South Africa, for which he had been awarded a grant from the Viking Fund, both because of his move from Oberlin to the University of Pennsylvania and his new responsibilities there, and because of his mother's illness. He finally returned the grant unused.

The years at Kansas and Oberlin, from 1937 to 1947, were Eiseley's most active period of anthropological research. Shortly after coming to

Kansas, he resumed field work, now concentrating more on archeology and physical anthropology than on vertebrate paleontology. At the Smith County site, Loren found evidence of a preceramic hunting culture that inhabited the Great Plains later than Folsom man (ca. 10,000 to 15,000 years ago) but earlier than the agricultural tribes who dwelt there from roughly 300 A.D. until the Spanish explorers arrived.[29] The value of the site, according to Eiseley, was that it established the presence of an early, bison-hunting culture during a period, approximately 7,000 to 8,000 years ago, when scientists presumed that the Plains were uninhabited. Eiseley believed that this area was continuously populated by small bands of nomadic hunters during the retreat of the last glaciers.

The results of his work were published in a series of scientific papers during the late 1930s and throughout the next decade. More importantly, Eiseley was experimenting with a form of the personal essay suitable for popular magazines. Perhaps his first piece in this mode, combining scientific information and personal recollection, was the essay entitled "Underground," which appeared in the October, 1937, issue of *Nebraska Alumnus*. It was later revised and adapted as part of chapter 10 ("The Crevice and the Eye") in *All the Strange Hours*.

The original sketch describes two archeologists who panic when the air gives out deep within a cave near Carlsbad, New Mexico, where they are searching for artifacts of Pleistocene man. As Eiseley notes in his introduction, "two men exploring an unknown cave . . . have a bit of luck that turns their possible tragedy into an adventure worth writing about." The archeologists discover a possible burial cairn while they are lost in the cave, although the narrator later realizes with a shudder that the body preserved there could have been his own. In the revised version, Eiseley turned this episode, by a kind of metaphoric compression, to a perspective dated ten thousand years in the past. Thus he emphasized man's insignificance in time. He makes the moment of insight occur as he and his partner realize that they are lost deep within the cave, squatting in the dark, "with an infinite distance to go." Contemporary man (represented by their guide, the genial priest who waits for them at the mouth of the cave) seems dwarfed and remote viewed up the tunnel of time. It is this insight, rather than the glimpse of the cairn, that the narrator now possesses as he emerges from the cave. Loren's prose would increasingly assume this metaphorical quality, especially in the essays he wrote during the late 1940s. These coalesced eventually to become *The Immense Journey*.

With "The Folsom Man," published in the December, 1942, *Scientific American*, Eiseley continued to experiment with his new expository form.

It let him "humanize" research by investing the essay with essentially poetic qualities of awe and wonder, and by expressing scientific concepts in a style so lucid that ordinary readers could easily understand. Further pieces in *Scientific American* and the *Prairie Schooner* followed, some probably excerpted from the discarded manuscript of "They Hunted the Mammoth." By the time Loren published his first essay in *Harper's,* "Long Ago Man of the Future," in January, 1947, he was evidently seeking a larger, more broadly cultivated audience, one with whom he could share joint interests in science and literature.

A sense of purpose also began to inform these essays, a sense he described in *All the Strange Hours* as the anthropologist's obligation to help men discover their past, observing that "only so can we learn our limitations and come in time to suffer life with compassion." That growing sense of purpose as a writer, together with a fortunate illness in the fall of 1948 that left him temporarily deaf and unable to teach for several months, inspired him to begin collecting the essays he had recently published in *Harper's, Scientific American,* and the *American Scholar,* and revising them with a book in mind. It was to be a book about the significance of evolution, cast in a series of original, highly imaginative essays: *The Immense Journey.* Although the book would not be published until he was almost fifty, he was already embarked on a new career as a literary naturalist.

Chapter Two
The Immense Journey:
The Making of a Literary Naturalist

"The most enormous extension of vision of which life is capable," writes Eiseley in *The Immense Journey,* "is the projection of itself into other lives." His first book-length work, published in 1957, is a carefully orchestrated series of such "extensions of vision," set within the controlling framework of evolution, that range forward and backward through time as they trace the emergence and development of life. Most of the thirteen chapters were originally published as separate essays and later rearranged to create a unified, imaginative account of how life evolved from its Precambrian origins to the magnificent complexity of man. The title of the book was inspired by a passage from Henri Frederic Amiel's *Journal Intime,* "It is as though the humanity of our day, had, like the migratory birds, an immense journey to make across space." Eiseley takes as his central theme speculations about man's recentness, his physical development, his genetic endowments, and the enormous, interwoven complexity of life.

First conceived during Eiseley's illness in 1948, *The Immense Journey* took almost ten years to complete. Many of the chapters first appeared in *Harper's,* the *American Scholar,* and *Scientific American,* but were revised as the book took shape.[1] In trying to unify these separate essays, Eiseley had difficulties with organization. As his book became more philosophical, he put aside sections already written. The title of the book changed at least three times and several publishers had turned Eiseley down before Hiram Haydn at Random House accepted the manuscript in 1956.[2] After eight years of negotiations, John Fischer of Harper and Brothers had decided that there would be an insufficient market for a collection of natural history essays.[3] Such fears seem misplaced in hindsight, since *The Immense Journey* has remained Eiseley's best-known work, selling over half a million copies in paperback and hardcover, with eight printings and over nine foreign translations. Haydn, as editor of the *American Scholar,* had enthusiastically published several of Eiseley's essays. When he joined Random House, he urged Eiseley to rework his essays in book form, with appropriate transitional links, rather than publish them as an essay collection.[4] Eiseley found the linking process difficult, but he persevered throughout the fall of 1956 and produced a manuscript substantially improved over earlier drafts. His subsequent books, as Haydn recalls, needed little or no revision.

Eiseley was fifty years old when *The Immense Journey* was published. Already a distinguished physical anthropologist and a respected teacher and administrator at the University of Pennsylvania, he was about to embark on a career as a literary naturalist and interpreter of science that would largely occupy the last twenty years of his life.

The Immense Journey

Though his first book to be published, *The Immense Journey* remains the touchstone for Eiseley's later accomplishments. Still the most popular of his books, it is also his work most accessible to the ordinary reader. Here the mature Eiseley voice first appears—scientifically informed, self-assured, and skeptical yet still personal in tone and capable of wonder and imagination. A subdued romantic, toughened by the rigors of his scientific training and by years of field research, he can respond with awe to the marvels and mysteries of the natural world. His observations and meditations are records of a personal journey in which he seeks "to understand and enjoy the miracles of this world, both in and out of science." Putting aside the once strict empiricism of science, Eiseley admits that he does not "pretend to set down, in Baconian terms, a true or even a consistent model of the universe." Instead, he proposes to offer "a bit of my personal universe," in terms as strange as those of the sixteenth-century geographic voyagers.

Eiseley conveys his musings with vivid, arresting images rather than abstract theories. His essays feature a variety of mammals, birds, and plants—fossil and living—set in dramatic landscapes of the past and present. They range through topics as diverse as the miracle of water, the appearance of flowering plants, the mechanisms of adaptations, and the mystery of the rapid emergence of the human brain. Several themes unify these speculations: an antimaterialistic bias, an opposition to scientism, and a desire to recover the past by using the imagination to transcend man's temporal restraints. Part of Eiseley's difficulty in organizing his account of man's "immense journey" was to find a narrative framework appropriate to such varied material: science, philosophy, poetry, and religion. Assistance from his editors enabled him to revise some of his published essays to form a continuous narrative within which he could explore the metaphor of evolutionary change as a series of "extensions of vision."

Time is the dimension through which evolution unfolds, and Eiseley continually uses metaphorical comparisons to broaden our understanding of the magnitude of the earth's geological age. We are prisoners of time—of the present moment—far more than we are prisoners of physical location.[5] Until we learn to perceive time and evolution in true perspective, we will not be able to see beyond the limits of a narrow anthropocentrism.

Evolution itself, the dominant theme of *The Immense Journey,* becomes "transcendental" in that all forms of life constantly strain against their limits, their ecological niches, in the quest for survival. Even the grotesque deep-sea fish "were all part of one of life's strangest qualities—its eternal dissatisfaction with what is, its persistent habit of reaching out into new environments and, by degrees, adapting itself to the most fantastic circumstances." Implied in these lesser extensions, moreover, is the ultimate mystery, man, who is himself in St. Augustine's words "a great deep." All the important Darwinian concepts—inheritance, variability, competition, natural selection, divergence, and extinction—are present in *The Immense Journey,* together with more recent discoveries about human evolution. Evolution becomes less a hypothesis, however, than a controlling metaphor to Eiseley, itself capable of manifold extensions and applications in the mind of a poet-scientist. To accept the idea of evolution is to accept a world of infinite possibility. Thus, for instance, in "The Flow of the River," an "evolutionary leap" is embodied in the actual leap of a channel catfish Eiseley had rescued from the frozen Platte River and kept for the rest of the winter in a fishtank, only to find the creature dead one morning on the basement floor.

The Immense Journey divides roughly into three major thematic sections: life before man (chapters 1–5), the emergence of man and his future prospects (chapters 6–10), and the mystery of life (chapters 11–13). In the first section, each chapter introduces at least one key evolutionary concept, beginning with Eiseley's discussion of evolutionary time in "The Slit," the significance of water as the medium of life in "The Flow of the River," the oceanic origins of life in "The Great Deeps," and the adaptability of fauna and flora in "The Snout" and "How Flowers Changed the World."

Chapters 4 and 5 introduce the mechanisms of evolutionary change. Eiseley shows how in each successive age the dominant forms arose from simpler animals that could make new adaptations because they were not restricted to a specific environment. Overspecialization often leads to extinction of a species when the conditions of life suddenly change. In the myth of the "snout," or Crossopterygian (a primitive fish), Eiseley recounts the epic story of how life first came ashore during the Devonian period. Thus he illustrates the concept of evolutionary succession (Cope's "law of the unspecialized") with a vivid and imaginative reconstruction of a prehistoric event.

The world we accept as "natural" today is actually the result of a series of complex adaptive responses made possible by the emergence of the angiosperms (flowering plants) less than a hundred million years ago. This new class of flora, with its nectar and wind-carried or insect-borne pollen, its fertilization within the flower, its fruits, its seed cases, and its elaborate transport mechanisms for those encased seeds—which Eiseley calls "life capsules"—made possible a series of parallel faunal adaptations. With nectar and pollen providing a new food source for them, insect varieties multiplied. The early mammals—Eiseley's "shabby little Paleocene rat"—now had the food to maintain their interior body temperatures at a consistently high level, which permitted the evolution of internal temperature regulation and correspondingly high metabolic rates. The fruits and seeds would also provide food for another evolving group of animals—the feathered lizards or birds. Thus angiosperms, mammals, insects, and birds all coevolved, as each in complex ways made the others' evolutionary success possible.

The next five chapters of *The Immense Journey,* beginning with "The Real Secret of Piltdown," deal with the emergence of man and his future prospects, an issue of particular interest to Eiseley as a physical anthropologist. Primate evolution was made possible by a series of climatic and ecological changes early in the Cenozoic era, some seventy million years ago. These changes did not ensure man's appearance or survival as a species, however. How man managed to emerge so quickly in evolutionary terms and to dominate his world so completely has been a matter of dispute among scientists for more than a century. Darwin and Wallace, for instance, offered quite different theories to account for man's success. Darwin argued for the slow and gradual evolution of *Homo sapiens* and believed that human evolution could be explained largely in terms of competition and natural selection. Wallace, on the other hand, believed that man emerged quite recently as a species. He saw unexplained forces at work in shaping human evolution, particularly in the rapid increase in the size of the human brain.

Although recent hominoid findings have supported Darwin's gradualist position and argued for a longer period of human development, Eiseley still rejected a strictly materialistic explanation of human evolution. He never accepted the implicit mind-matter dualism of science, which left an unaccountable gap between matter and consciousness. There were too many unresolved questions, he believed, for man to trace the development of consciousness entirely through mechanistic causes. Nor could he satisfy himself that the "creativity" of natural selection alone could explain man's uniqueness or his cultural achievements. Instead, Eiseley and Wallace both emphasized cultural rather than biological evolution in explaining man's distinctiveness.

These contrasting views of evolution have profoundly different implications in terms of human nature. A "pure" Darwinism seemed, to the Victorians at least, to sanction human aggression as justifiable or even beneficial from an evolutionary perspective. Darwin's critics argued that natural selection condemned man to endless struggle, with the strong and ruthless surviving. This view of human nature has been used to rationalize all manner of oppression and injustice and to minimize man's artistic ability and his altruistic impulses. Darwin insisted that these cultural accomplishments could be explained in biological terms, whereas Wallace argued that natural selection and the struggle for existence could not alone have produced man's artistic, mathematical, and musical abilities. Nor did man's increased brain size automatically make him civilized, since his brain capacity probably increased before he was fully able to use it: if indeed he can fully use it yet.

Much of the problem for anthropologists arises from the lack of a reliable fossil record for early man. Unlike the remarkably complete paleontological evidence for the evolution of the horse, the evidence of human evolution is at best fragmentary and incomplete. Entire theories have been based on a few disarticulated bones. With so little information available it seems premature to speculate about the physical development of man. Eiseley particularly opposed the reductionistic implications of a strict Darwinism that deny our intangible but uniquely human qualities. As he demonstrates in his conclusion to "The Real Secret of Piltdown," the most important result of the discovery of this hoax was to force scientists to reconsider their assumptions about the development of the human brain.

In the next chapter, Eiseley compares our evolutionary past to a "maze," a confusing network of descent from our tarsioid or anthropoid ancestors with no clear evolutionary pattern. Natural history is a labyrinth from which we draw subjective impressions of human nature. Like the witches in _Macbeth_, it confirms what we wish to see in ourselves. This confusion is reflected in the debate among scientists about man's origins. Some imagine man as descended from a "homunculus," or "little man," while others regard his ancestor as a "shaggy anthropoid" or "apeman." Eiseley finds insufficient evidence for a clear verdict either way. As he notes in an unused epigraph taken from Henri Bergson's _Creative Evolution,_ "the route we pursue in time is strewn with the remains of all that we began to be, of all that we might have become."[6] What interests Eiseley most is the combination of physiological and anatomical adaptations that mark human evolution: bipedal locomotion, prehensile hands, color vision, stereoscopic (front-set) eyes, prolonged infancy, and expanded brain size. These physical changes, in turn, made advances in human culture possible, such as man's use of tools and weapons, the discovery of fire, and the development of agriculture through the domestication of certain plants and animals.

Man is what Eiseley calls a "dream animal" because he was able to use the evolutionary advantage of his enlarged brain to develop symbolic communication—language—and through words to attain self-consciousness and memory. With man, life had at last become aware of itself. In a hauntingly beautiful passage, Eiseley describes this mythic moment of man's departure from the "Eden" of the instinctual world to the awesome knowledge of self: "For the first time in four billion years a living creature had contemplated himself and heard with a sudden, unaccountable loneliness, the whisper of the wind in the night reeds. Perhaps he knew, there in the grass by the chill waters, that he had before him an immense journey" (125–26). The story of Eden becomes here an allegorical account of man's passage from the certainty of instinct to the vast, uncertain world of knowledge, self-consciousness, and choice.

In "Man of the Future," Eiseley dismisses predictions about man's future appearance by demonstrating that they would not be new. An extinct line of early African anthropoids, the "Boscop Man," possessed these same "ultramodern" features—a large cranium and skull volume, a high forehead, small teeth, and delicate, childlike features. Yet the Boscop people disappeared, perhaps unable to compete with aggressive neighbors or, more likely, because they did not develop a sustaining culture. Their brain size, though larger than that of modern man, apparently went unused. Again Eiseley stresses the importance of cultural rather than physical features in defining human nature.

"Little Men and Flying Saucers" continues Eiseley's discussion of man's physical and cultural uniqueness. Man was neither "prefigured" in earlier forms of life or in the pattern of creation, nor is he likely to find his counterpart anywhere else in the universe. He is the solitary and particular creation of a set of biological conditions unlikely ever to be duplicated. To believe otherwise is to indulge in the conceit of a man-centered universe, whether we believe that previous forms of life point toward man or that the human drama unfolds on other worlds. Man's prospects, according to Eiseley, are not buried in the past or hidden in some obscure future, but lie within himself, latent, in the dreams and visions he projects onto the world.

Since the narrative perspective of *The Immense Journey* continually moves from the specific toward the abstract, it is appropriate that the final three chapters—the section on "the mystery of life"—contain a philosophical summation. Here Eiseley offers what might almost be called a "vitalistic" affirmation of life. In each of these chapters he asserts opposition to scientistic assumptions that account for life entirely in chemical or physical terms, or else view living creatures as nothing more than complex, sentient machines. Through a series of visionary moments Eiseley shows how repugnant such a philosophy was to him—in the soaring of pigeons above a city street, the reanimation of inert chemicals in a flight of warblers over the Badlands, the cry of the song sparrows against "Cain" the raven, the heroism of the spider, and the reunion of the hawks—all eloquent replies to the reductionism of science. For some readers these passages might seem sentimental, but the emotional conviction in these anecdotes always points beyond itself to some broader though unstated meaning. It is never cultivated for its own sake. Evolution becomes such a potent metaphor in Eiseley's work because through it he implies that there is something mysterious, purposeful, even transcendent about these apparently random events in the natural world.

In "The Secret of Life," Eiseley suggests that, having displaced the biblical creation myth, contemporary science is obliged to create a mythology of its own to answer the ultimate questions. Though insisting upon the inscrutability of life, he hints that its "secret" may be contained in the ability of living organisms to reproduce their precise pattern, structure, and form through genetic codes. For him, the living creature is always greater than the sum of its parts. Reductive analysis and an "uncompromising materialism" will not yield the secret of the creation of even the simplest one-celled organisms from their constituent molecules.

Clearly a romantic and perhaps even a vitalist at this point, he hopes that the secret of life will continue to elude the men in the laboratory. Eiseley then compares the mystery of organic form to a "dance of the molecules," a metaphor that calls to mind the graceful patterns and configurations of living structure, as well as the dominant Renaissance symbol for the harmony of the universe, found in Sir John Davies's poem "Orchestra." His appreciation of the patterns of nature is finally more aesthetic and religious than analytic, so that *The Immense Journey* ends on a note of unorthodox science, with Eiseley's affirmation of the potential for life contained in all matter:

Rather, I would say that if "dead" matter has reared up this curious landscape of fiddling crickets, song sparrows, and wondering men, it must be plain even to the most devoted materialist that the matter of which he speaks contains amazing, if not dreadful powers, and may not impossibly be, as Hardy has suggested, "but one mask of many worn by the Great Face behind." (210)

The Victorian Naturalist

Dissatisfied with the restrictive, value-free orientation of modern science, Eiseley turned to the essay in hope of finding a form through which he could articulate his sense of wonder. For some time he had been privately disillusioned with the "religion of science," with its rigid assumption that every natural event in the universe can be rationally explained by prior events. He found it increasingly difficult to reconcile his "private universe" of mystery and beauty with the rational universe of science, where everything was ultimately reducible to fact and measurement. No longer did he wish to maintain the scientific detachment that would not permit an imaginative or aesthetic response to his study of early man. "I no longer believe that science will save the world," he commented in one of his notebooks.

"Anthropology," Eiseley once wrote, "is the science of man eternally trying to understand himself and never succeeding." He envisioned anthropology as a human science, admitting a variety of styles and approaches, yet he found himself dismissed by his colleagues as a "popularizer" or a writer of "inspirational literature."[7] Faced with this kind of determined hostility to his imaginative style, Eiseley turned from conventional science to a form of personal expression more compatible with his sensibility, that of the literary naturalist. In "The Judgment of the Birds," he describes his purpose as a seeker of "natural revelations" for a culture that has lost its sense of wonder:

> It is a commonplace of all religious thought, even the most primitive, that the man seeking visions and insight must go apart from his fellows and live for a time in the wilderness. If he is of the proper sort, he will return with a message. It may not be a message from the god he set out to seek, but even if he has failed in that particular, he will have had a vision or seen a marvel, and these are always worth listening to and thinking about. (163)

These essays would appeal less to the narrow interest of the specialist than to "those who have retained a true sense for the marvellous, and who are capable of discerning in the ordinary flow of events the point at which the mundane world gives way to quite another dimension."

With this change of orientation, Eiseley placed himself in a long and rich tradition of English and American natural history writers—including Gilbert White, Richard Jefferies, W. H. Hudson, Ralph Waldo Emerson, and Henry David Thoreau. Each of these writers, though prescientific, recorded his impressions of nature in a precise, distinctive, personal style. Although obviously related to an older pastoral tradition, natural history writing differs by avoiding the sentimentality, the stock nature descriptions, and the "pathetic fallacy" typical of literary pastoralism. Instead, the natural history essay gains vividness and accuracy from the influence of empirical science. It is both personal and factual, balancing objectivity with delight. Yet the literature of natural history and modern scientific writing are also distinguishable in several important ways. The essence of science is to be quantitative and experimental in approach, whereas the art of natural history is to observe, appreciate, and record natural phenomena as they appear. This is not to deny the importance of observation in science, since a discovery often begins with the recognition of "broken symmetry," when a scientist notes the exception in the pattern. But science extends beyond observation to the making and testing of hypotheses.

In "The Enchanted Glass," Eiseley eloquently defines the borders between literature and science.[8] The study of nature can either be factual or contemplative, depending upon the mindset of the person involved. Eiseley compares the two mindsets, finding the Baconian "severely experimental, unaesthetic and empirical" and its opposite "literary, personal and contemplative." Then he shows how they differ in attitude and purpose: the scientific attempting to discover the "underlying laws" that govern the natural world, and the contemplative seeking to record personal responses to that world. Description and analysis alone cannot provide a full understanding of the natural world, according to Eiseley, because "when the human mind exists in the light of reason, and no more than reason, we may say with certainty that man and all that made him will be in that instant gone." There is also a need for contemplative natural history, an approach that "contains overtones of thought which is not science, nor intended to be, and yet without which science itself would be poorer." Contemplative natural history offers what Eiseley calls "a natural history of the soul." This human response to the world is especially important, he notes, in an age that does not lend itself to contemplation. A third approach is also possible, however. Besides straightforward science and contemplative natural history, there is a more personalized scientific literature that reflects a labor of love, where fact and knowledge are balanced by affection. Eiseley valued both these approaches for their "synthesis of knowledge and emotional insight."

The natural history writer is primarily interested in recording his aesthetic response to the natural world. As an outdoorsman or field naturalist, he shows a general interest in the birds, animals, plants, and insects of his native region. Always he cultivates an affectionate sense of locale, an appreciation of a particular physical landscape, whether it be White's Selborne, Jefferies's Swindon, Hudson's pampas, Emerson's Concord, or Thoreau's Walden. The world of the natural history writer appears through the medium of a distinct personality, a recognizable "voice," while the modern scientist strives to maintain strict objectivity, refining the observer out of existence. This "myth" of complete scientific objectivity, epistemologically dubious, has encouraged the writing of scientific papers in dull, lifeless prose that is supposed to appear unbiased and detached. Yet one cannot efface point of view so long as there is a person doing the observing or recording the data.

This dry, passive scientific style is the antithesis of art—it is the voice of men without faces or personalities, an echo from the dissecting room. Fortunately there are now alternatives to this "official" style of science, due in large degree to the influence of such articulate spokesmen for science as Eiseley, Jacob Bronowski, Robert Jastrow, and Lewis Thomas—men not hesitant to express their ideas through a personal medium. Many of them have returned to the natural history essay or other varieties of the essay form as a way of expressing their response to their work—their delight and pleasure—in an informal but accurate manner.

Not that Eiseley was an apostate scientist; it was simply that he could not express what he felt most deeply within the framework of the impersonal scientific style. In *The Dignity and Advancement of Learning,* Sir Francis Bacon classified scientists in two general categories, the "miners" (or researchers) and the "smiths" (or refiners). Eiseley was clearly one of the latter, gifted with a synthesizing, metaphoric mind that constantly sought connections between fact and imagination. He possessed the poetic vision to perceive the natural history of life's emergence as an epic event—a spectacle of prehistory—heretofore described in flat, expository language, but capable of being recast as a literary narrative. But it took a special kind of talent to accomplish this, one more akin to the Victorian literary naturalist than the modern specialist, someone not intimidated by the "two cultures" division or the fear of bridging disciplines. Eiseley, of course, had long been pursuing separate careers as a poet and a scientist, with the hope of eventually combining them in some literary form. Now the personal essay seemed best to fulfill that promise for him. As Eiseley commented to a colleague's inquiry about encouraging good writing among scientists: "I always had a joint interest in English literature and science so that the 'two culture problem' never concerned me and I was never conscious of it except to the degree that I have been castigated by nonliterary colleagues in science."[9]

Although C. P. Snow blamed the "two culture" crisis largely on literary intellectuals' unwillingness or inability to master basic scientific principles, the issue is really more complicated than that.[10] The split is of recent origin, caused in part by the proliferation of science and the explosion of scientific knowledge. The ideal of a common culture has given way to a range of specialized audiences—literary and scientific—with few overlapping interests. The contemporary scientist necessarily addresses his peers, rather than a general public. The Victorian scientist, on the other hand, had to be a man of letters because he wrote for a general rather than a specialized audience—one he could not depend upon to extract his argument from his charts and diagrams if his prose was murky or obscure. Darwin, Wallace, Huxley—the Victorian scientists and writers whom Eiseley so much admired—mastered the gift of expressing complex ideas simply in order to reach their audiences, who were skeptical of evolutionary theory. These men spoke for themselves, Eiseley reminds us, "not as a team, not as a committee." Even Darwin's prose, so ponderous in places, often surprises the reader with passages of vivid imagery and persuasive skill. The study of natural history was respected by these men, who were not constrained by our mania for specialization. As Eiseley notes in *The Night Country*:

Even though they were not discoverers in the objective sense, one feels at times that the great nature essayists had more individual perception than their scientific contemporaries. Theirs was a different contribution. They opened the minds of men by the sheer power of their thought. The world of nature, once seen through the eye of genius, is never seen in quite the same manner afterward. A dimension has been added, something that lies beyond the careful analysis of professional biology. (142)

In many ways, Eiseley resembles these gifted Victorians, naturalists with a literary bent, who forever changed man's understanding of his place in the natural world. An eloquent example of Victorian science is Thomas H. Huxley's *On a Piece of Chalk,* a lecture on geological time and evolution given in 1868 to the workingmen of Norwich. Eiseley's introduction to a recent edition of Huxley's lecture reveals much about his divided loyalty between literature and science.[11] He speaks of "the two faces" of Huxley—the honest and tireless champion of science, and the driven, defeated man "rendered intellectually impotent before space, time, and the unknowable." Like Huxley, Eiseley retained throughout his life "a lingering poetic eloquence, a fondness for the literary essay turned to scientific purposes." He praises Huxley and Agassiz, two men who disagreed about evolution, but who, because they agreed about "the necessity of writing lucidly upon scientific subjects for the layman shared a common tradition."

Even in his thematic concerns Eiseley shares much with these Victorian naturalists. As in the case of their work, time and evolution have been the dominant themes in virtually everything he has written. But unlike Darwin, Eiseley is not writing cautiously to introduce a disturbing and even heretical theory bearing on man's origins. Instead he is exploring the poetic implications of the evolutionary metaphor through a series of visionary extensions in time, imaginatively re-creating those natural events that led to the emergence of man; but his terms are far more tempered and compassionate than Tennyson's "nature, red in tooth and claw." Still, there is something distinctively Victorian about Eiseley's intellectual temperament and his dominant interest in the history of life and its implications for what Bronowski optimistically called "the ascent of man." Eiseley was not so confident of the direction this evolutionary metaphor suggested—if indeed man's evolution had direction or purpose—but if it was an "ascent," then it was a movement toward greater compassion and kinship with all forms of life, rather than simply an advance in technological and manipulative skill.

The Concealed Essay

Despite these affinities with Victorian men of science, it would be a mistake to view Eiseley's work as derivative or anachronistic. His visionary power, his animistic descriptions, and the range of his philosophical speculations distinguish him from his Victorian predecessors. Eiseley is less optimistic about the prospects of science than either Darwin or Huxley, so that a sense of diminishment pervades his work. A strong romantic tendency reinforces this pessimistic tone, particularly in his various self-dramatizations: as the neglected child, the impoverished student, the wandering bone hunter, the midnight scholar, the weary insomniac. While this attitude is largely temperamental, it may also reflect, especially in his most melancholic or somber moods, the influence of his diverse reading—Edgar Allan Poe, Robert Burton, and Sir Thomas Browne. It may also be the mood in our time.

As an undergraduate at Nebraska, Eiseley had studied the nineteenth-century essay under Professor Kenneth Forward, who may have been the source of Eiseley's later remark that "there are no perfect essays, only well-composed ones." Throughout his life, his favorite authors remained Coleridge, Hazlitt, De Quincey, Lamb, Francis Bacon, and Sir Thomas Browne—all masters of the essay who loved obscure and arcane references; elegant practitioners of an ornate style who emphasized tone and mood in their writing. Eiseley may have learned from Bacon the habit of balancing scientific or scholarly ideas with vivid metaphors, although in this respect he is far more candid than Bacon, especially when he mentions the troubled and painful memories of his childhood. Retaining Bacon's philosophical sweep and scientific vision, Eiseley tempers it with a baroque, introspective style more reminiscent of Robert Burton, Thomas Browne, Abraham Cowley, and the later Thoreau. Certainly Eiseley shared Browne's interest in quaint and antiquarian lore, with its emphasis on the remote and mysterious, though Browne also served as an intriguing model of what Eiseley called "a great amphibian," a man of science who was able to retain his religious faith.

Each of these writers cultivated the essay in its purest form, as a mode of personal expression. Edmund Fuller has observed that "the word 'essay' is derived from *'essai'*—a noun from a verb—the *attempt* to express oneself, in brief and highly personal terms, on some single subject."[12] Montaigne developed this prose form in the sixteenth century as a medium for what Fuller calls "reflective speculation and self-examination," and Francis Bacon subsequently introduced it into the English literary tradition with the brilliant and concise formulations in his *Essays,* first published in 1597. The essay found a ready audience through the eighteenth-century newspaper, beginning with the *Tatler* and the *Spectator.* Under the influence of Johnson, Goldsmith, and Chesterfield, the essay became a reasoned, reflective form, though it remained for the romantic writers to expand the scope of the essay as a personal or familiar form.

What Eiseley accomplished is virtually to invent a new genre—an imaginative synthesis of literature and science—one that enlarged the power and range of the personal essay. Eiseley, who was remarkably learned and well-read, a lifelong antiquarian and lover of old books, found the personal or familiar essay the most congenial form through which he could express his wide range of interests. The "literary essay turned to scientific purposes" offered the ideal mode for such self-discoveries as he wished to offer, modest and unassuming, tentative and speculative without appearing dogmatic. Eiseley's style, though distinctive, seems to echo the ornate, mannered form of the seventeenth-century prose writers.

Eiseley's mastery of the personal essay developed gradually. As he explains in *All the Strange Hours,* he returned to the familiar essay in the late 1940s after "a scientifically oriented magazine which had requested an article from me upon man's evolution reneged in favor of a more distinguished visitor to America." Eiseley then decided to rework the rejected essay in a more literary fashion—"into what I now term the *concealed essay* [italics mine], in which personal anecdote was allowed gently to bring under observation thoughts of a more purely scientific nature." The "concealed essay" starts with a vivid anecdote or reminiscence and gradually expands it in a scientific or contemplative direction. The subject matter of the essay, whatever it may be, is framed or "concealed" by the personal approach, which serves as a rhetorical device to engage the reader's attention. Thus the "concealed essay" becomes for Eiseley a highly elaborate form, with frequent literary references and allusions, numerous quotations, multiple themes, and an interwoven structure of contemplative concerns. This casual and informal, though sophisticated technique brings narrative and personal experience—essentially fictional and autobiographical tools—to bear on what is otherwise simply expository material—scientific fact and hypothesis. Eiseley justifies his style as adding personal interest without distorting the accuracy of the scientific material:

That the self and its minute adventures may be interesting every essayist from Montaigne to Emerson has intimated, but only if one is utterly, nakedly honest and does not pontificate. In a silence which nothing could impinge, I shifted away from the article as originally intended. A personal anecdote introduced it, personal matter lay scattered through it, personal philosophy concluded it, and yet I had done no harm to the scientific data. (178)

Thus the familiar essay points out the connections between things that seem quite disparate. Beginning with a specific setting or thematic description, it creates a dramatic occasion and then dramatizes the self in that occasion. It takes the reader on an intellectual journey and returns him with new insights. Along the way it maintains the voice of informed conversation on a common theme, blending literature, science, religion, and philosophy—a whole range of gratuitous information that demonstrates the common ground among seemingly unrelated topics, and allows the reader to see for himself how they relate.

This approach may have been first suggested by Eiseley's anthropology lectures at Kansas, where he was teaching a variety of courses in new subject areas. One of the lecture techniques he devised was to enliven his presentations by drawing upon his field experiences and using them to illustrate his more abstract material. The same balance of the personal and the scientific distinguishes Eiseley's mature style. Part of his accomplishment as a writer is that his essays seem so artless, when, as he acknowledges in his autobiography, they were actually so highly contrived:

In all the questioning about what makes a writer, and especially perhaps the personal essayist, I have seen little reference to this fact; namely, that the brain has become a kind of unseen artist's loft. There are pictures that hang askew, pictures with the outlines barely chalked in, pictures torn, pictures the artist has striven unsuccessfully to erase, pictures that only emerge and glow in a certain light. They have all been teleported, stolen, as it were, out of time. They represent no longer the sequential flow of ordinary memory. They can be pulled about on easels, examined within the mind itself. The act is not one of total recall like that of the professional mnemonist. Rather it is the use of things extracted from their context in such a way that they have become the unique possession of a single life. The writer sees back to these transports alone, bare, perhaps few in number, but endowed with a symbolic life. He cannot obliterate them. He can only drag them about, magnify or reduce them as his artistic sense dictates, or juxtapose them in order to enhance a pattern. One thing he cannot do. He cannot destroy what will not be destroyed; he cannot determine in advance what will enter his mind. (151)

What Eiseley has given us here is a formula for his work, a glimpse into the mind of the writer at work, and a statement of the forces that compelled him to write. The principle operating here seems to be a "reenactment through memory," a heightened and dramatized account of past moments of intensified experience that eventually led to new and startling insights.

Memory, landscape, and visual imagination combine to shape many of Eiseley's most powerful narrative passages. When the reader turns to the first chapter of *The Immense Journey,* he immediately senses a powerful eidetic imagination at work, a method of composition, as Eiseley has noted, through "the pictures that haunt my head." In "The Slit" this visual imagination freely moves from the present landscape, the bleak uplands of western Nebraska, to a vertical escarpment, which serves as the point of departure for a metaphoric journey backward in time, accentuated by Eiseley's chance discovery of a primitive mammal's skull, staring at him, embedded in the sandstone wall. That moment of discovery, in turn, serves as the impetus for a second metaphoric leap, an imaginative extension backward to the early Tertiary period, where "cat and man and weasel must leap into a single shape" in a common ancestor. While Eiseley chips away at the fossil skull, a third metaphoric transition takes place as he becomes aware of the marvelous dexterity of his fingers—"the human hand that has been fin and scaly reptile foot and furry paw." Using the poetic device of the synecdoche, a substitution of the part for the whole, he achieves a remarkable compression of time, and, through the leap of his imagination from fact to symbol, he emphasizes the fortuitous chance that marks so much of evolutionary change.

Every image, every transition is carefully selected throughout this essay to remind us of the enormous role of chance and contingency along the road of that vast "caravan" in time that has produced man. Time remains, in Eiseley's words, "a dimension denied man," but one that he may yet learn to comprehend, through the powers of the scientific imagination. Most importantly, though, the prehistoric past serves for Eiseley as a symbol of something remote and unreachable, a "middle border" of awe and wonder, a tonic to the jaded imagination. There is scarcely another writer for whom the remote, geological past is so imaginatively vivid as it is for him.

Eiseley recognized that the concept of geological time is one of the most difficult scientific notions for the ordinary person to comprehend. As he was to argue later in *The Firmament of Time,* "we have difficulty in visualizing the age-old processes involved in the upheaval of mountain systems, the advance of continental glaciations or the creation of life." Less than two hundred years have passed since the discovery of the vast age of the earth. Thus, in *The Immense Journey,* Eiseley was forced to devise a new mode of visionary natural history to convey his impression of the protean quality of life as viewed from a geological perspective. In his imaginative synthesis of literature and science, he combines narrative and hypothesis, fact and feeling, metaphor and exposition. The result is a new style of scientific literature, and a new literary genre, an expansion of the personal essay for scientific purposes.

Reception of *The Immense Journey*

In an important passage from "The Slit," Eiseley speaks of being restrained by the conventional methods of science because they do not allow adequate freedom to express his sense of the miraculous in the natural world. As he often implies in wry anecdotes about the disapproval of some of his colleagues, Eiseley recognizes the scientific method as a kind of contemporary orthodoxy, which he threatens, as Bacon had in his attack on medieval scholasticism, by questioning its scope and limitations. As Eiseley warns his readers repeatedly, he is not a spokesman for conventional science. Instead, he is a poet-shaman, a wizard-alchemist who adopts the disguise of a changeling and calls his reverence and compassion for life "scientific" for the sake of his professional reputation. In another early essay, "Obituary of a Bone Hunter," later reprinted in *The Night Country,* he explains that in a series of three temptations, which our age would call "opportunities," he refused the possibility of fame and reputation to protect another living creature or to maintain his personal integrity. Even in this early essay, his composure over the loss of fame suggests the philosophical direction his work would take, in which the insight or idea becomes more important than the physical artifact. In each of the three incidents, he gives up his quest to find evidence of early man in North America. The reasons why he turns away from these promising sites have little to do with the potential value of the finds. Each time there was some personal scruple that could not be violated: a fear of spiders in close quarters, an unwillingness to disturb an owl's nest, and a refusal to cooperate with the demands of an eccentric.

Given Eiseley's explicit literary intentions and his repeated disavowals of conventional science, it is not surprising that some of his colleagues in anthropology were skeptical about his work, but the lack of literary recognition for his accomplishments as an essayist and a prose stylist is more difficult to explain. Book reviewers of his work have generally been enthusiastic, and his essays have been widely reprinted and anthologized, but Eiseley has still received relatively little serious critical attention.[13] One of the few exceptions to this neglect has been Van Wyck Brooks's tribute, in the last volume of his autobiography, *In the Shadow of the Mountain: My Post-Meridian Years:*

I have long believed that the best writers are now the writers of natural history who are ignored commonly in critical circles because they are concerned with permanent things outside of the changing human world that interests the novelists and most of the poets. . . . Otherwise there would be no writers more critically esteemed than Henry Beston or Rachel Carson or Loren Eiseley, who has related, in *The Immense Journey,* the ascent of man from his dark stairwell. Why are these writers of natural history now called popularizers of science as if their style went for nothing, as if this were the bottom rung of the ladder of science instead of an upper rung of the ladder of art?[14]

Brooks is undoubtedly correct in his assessment of the lack of critical interest in natural history writers. Yet *The Immense Journey* and his subsequent books have enjoyed so wide a readership that Eiseley is assured a prominent place among such modern natural history writers as Aldo Leopold, Joseph Wood Krutch, Marston Bates, and Annie Dillard, all accomplished stylists who blend their natural descriptions with acute philosophical observations. Eiseley's literary success may also have encouraged other scientists, such as Carl Sagan and Stephen Jay Gould, to write for a popular audience.

The years following *The Immense Journey* were active and hectic ones for a man as shy and reserved as Eiseley, and he sometimes felt uncomfortable in the role of public figure. For eleven years he had been curator of early man at the University Museum, and in 1959 he was appointed provost of the University of Pennsylvania, an administrative position he found so uncongenial that he resigned within two years. He was then named Benjamin Franklin Professor of Anthropology and the History of Science, a position that largely freed him from teaching and administrative responsibilities in order to write. Yet Eiseley also relished the increased contact with the public his reputation brought. Among his many activities he prepared the opening article for the *Saturday Evening Post* "Adventures of the Mind" series, and later hosted an NBC-TV children's series, "Animal Secrets," that ran for two seasons.[15] During this time he also maintained an enormous personal correspondence with the aid of his secretary, Mrs. Caroline Werkley, with whose assistance he thoughtfully and graciously answered countless letters from his readers and viewers. But his intellectual interests, as evidenced by *Darwin's Century,* seemed to be shifting increasingly to the history and philosophy of science.

Chapter Three
Evolution: The History of an Idea

"I have made no great discoveries," writes Eiseley in "Obituary of a Bone Hunter," in regard to his uneventful field research, "I'm the man who didn't find the skull." While these comments express his regret in not finding substantial evidence of early man in North America, there were other areas of scholarship available to Eiseley to compensate for this disappointment. Besides publishing his popular essays, he became active with a number of professional organizations during the 1950s, including the Wenner-Gren Foundation and the American Philosophical Society. As the first president of the American Institute of Human Paleontology, Eiseley traveled to London in 1951 to purchase F. O. Barlow's extensive collection of fossil molds of early man, and had these casts, along with Barlow's files of his business correspondence, transferred to the University Museum in Philadelphia, where Eiseley served as curator of early man.[1] There he arranged to have the casting program continue at the Museum and produce replicas of the most important anthropoid fossil remains.

With his strong interest in Victorian science, Eiseley was delighted when in 1951 the American Philosophical Society in Philadelphia acquired a major collection of Darwin papers, the Darwin-Lyell correspondence. At the request of William E. Lingelbach, Society librarian, he assisted in the expansion of the Darwin Collection by searching bookstores and contacting book dealers for rare volumes related to Darwiniana and the history of evolution and natural selection. These activities reflected his growing interest in the history of science and his enthusiasm for rare books, particularly those related to early science and natural history. In recognition of his bibliographic work and the three papers he contributed to the *Proceedings,* Eiseley was elected a member of the American Philosophical Society in 1960.[2]

Eiseley's familiarity with the Darwin Collection at the American Philosophical Society soon proved useful for another scholarly project. Early in the 1950s, an editor from Doubleday and Company contacted him about writing a carefully researched study of the Darwinian epoch. Eiseley decided to begin this book even while he was trying to complete *The Immense Journey*, though it meant investing scholarly effort in the one task and creative energies in the other. He would acknowledge in his autobiography that *Darwin's Century* was largely intellectual detective work, much of it conducted in the cramped, overheated stacks of the old Furness Library at the University of Pennsylvania. While Eiseley was busy compiling this material, he immersed himself so thoroughly in the Victorian milieu that his wife once remarked absentmindedly when someone telephoned for him, "Darwin will not be home to lunch." Preparation of *Darwin's Century* took more than five years, busy years when Eiseley was also chairman of both the Anthropology Department and the Faculty Senate. A grant from the Wenner-Gren Foundation enabled him to take a sabbatical leave during the 1952–53 academic year, but after that he worked evenings, weekends, and summers to finish the book in time for publication in 1959, the centennial year of *The Origin of Species*. Critical response to *Darwin's Century* was impressive. The book won the National Phi Beta Kappa Science Prize for 1959 and the Athenaeum Society of Philadelphia Literary Award for best nonfiction book of the year in 1960.

Darwin's Century

Darwin's Century is probably the most difficult book for the casual reader of Eiseley's works. Closely reasoned and expository, it is the most scholarly and least personal of his books, devoted almost exclusively to tracing the emergence of a scientific concept in one of the most exacting of fields, the history of ideas. Though densely written and without the imaginative appeal of Eiseley's other books, *Darwin's Century* is a substantial intellectual history, based on diligent research and impeccable scholarship. As such, it records another of Eiseley's major interests, his preoccupation with the history of science, particularly the history of the idea of biological evolution. As a book collector and antiquarian with a special affection for rare editions of early scientific works and natural history, Eiseley sorted carefully through the publications of Darwin's predecessors for hints of the idea of evolution, long evident in scientific writing before Darwin. Even erroneous beliefs, such as catastrophism and progressionism, recognized that life had changed and that certain forms of life had become extinct through the course of time. Earlier scientists like Buffon, Lamarck, and Erasmus Darwin had discussed the possibility of organic evolution. Darwinian precursors particularly interested Eiseley because he believed that advancement in science is a collective enterprise and that the great minds of an age never work in intellectual isolation. Newton recognized that he saw further than most men only because he stood on the shoulders of giants. So it had been, Eiseley believed, with Darwin and the emergence of the theory of biological evolution. The subtitle of *Darwin's Century—Evolution and the Men Who Discovered It*—reflects his thesis.

"The recovery of the lost history of the earth," according to Eiseley, was a scientific achievement comparable to the discovery of the New World. The original title for his study had been *The Time Voyagers,* and Eiseley continually used metaphors of voyage and exploration to trace the series of early scientific discoveries that prepared the way for "Darwin's century." Given the complexity of the evolutionary hypothesis, the entire Christian world view had to be altered before the notions of illimitable time and biological change could be accepted. So radical a change in outlook was slow to occur, even after the Copernican revolution. It could happen only after the requisite insights and evidence had been patiently assembled in several different scientific fields, notably geology, taxonomy, morphology, and comparative anatomy, and after the correct conclusions had been drawn from this new information. But first the accepted Christian view had to be liberalized and a static conception of nature had to become dynamic. Eiseley devotes twelve chapters to the events that led to Darwin's discovery, to the elaboration and clarification of evolutionary doctrine after its initial reception, and to the series of scientific challenges Darwin faced, particularly in describing the descent of man. After Darwin, Eiseley traces the development of Darwinism to the end of the nineteenth century. His proposed second volume, *After Darwin's Century,* was never completed.

Eiseley's central perception in *Darwin's Century* was that the new intellectual discovery gradually emerged from the prevailing climate of ideas and became in turn the essence of the succeeding intellectual atmosphere. Scientific ideas had for Eiseley the tangibility of objects, and he had the knack of dealing lucidly with difficult abstractions. Since ideas have their genesis and evolution within a culture, Eiseley proposed to refine our understanding of how the concept of organic evolution was developed from its origins in eighteenth-century science to its fulfillment in the theory of natural selection. Thus his account begins in the "fossil world" of lost documents and records of Darwin's predecessors and leads through intellectual labyrinths beneath pre-Darwinian science to *The Origin of Species.* Eiseley examines the growth of a set of ideas in Western science, rather than the lives or personalities of the men who discovered them. Later he was to temper the austerity of this approach when he reworked much of the thematic material in *Darwin's Century* for the vivid essays in *The Firmament of Time*.

Darwin's Forerunners

In *Darwin's Century*, Eiseley identifies two approaches to the reconstruction of the history of life: through the study of living organisms and through fossil records. Using the Baconian method, early scientists turned their attention to the natural world and began to question inherited assumptions of Aristotelian science and church doctrine. In particular, they began to doubt the validity of the medieval "Great Chain of Being," which presupposed a hierarchy of life, but in a fixed and unchanging order. Despite this reevaluation, however, there were still a number of obstacles in the way of a true evolutionary theory: the idea of the fixity of species, the lack of knowledge in comparative anatomy, taxonomy, and morphology, the presumed short age-span of the earth, the lack of a theory of geological change, the absence of an adequate fossil record, the need to place fossils in stratigraphic sequence, the assumption that the struggle for existence was a conservative, pruning force rather than a creative force, and the disbelief in extinction. Pre-Darwinian scientists had to resolve these issues before a comprehensive evolutionary theory was possible. Eighteenth-century science sought reason, order, and permanence in the world through the discovery of natural laws. Their universe was stable and self-balancing. Nature was the second great "book of revelation," and "natural theology" expressed the harmony between nature and religion. Yet this fixed and stable order was soon to dissolve before the turbulent forces of the romantic movement, which brought the theory of organic change to government, science, and religion.

New discoveries in geology and paleontology, in particular, made an evolutionary theory possible because they expanded or "naturalized" the reach of time far beyond the framework of biblical chronology. Eiseley compares the knowledge of the true age of the earth to a "pirate chart," with several pre-Darwinian scientists holding pieces of the chart but none before Charles Lyell having the complete map. Once reports of fossil discoveries began to circulate, various "catastrophist" theories arose, all postulating divine intervention in the form of a series of "special creations," in an attempt to explain fossil remains and their implied evidence of extinction. Each separate layer of life was supposed to have been annihilated by a great deluge or some other natural catastrophe documented in the Old Testament. The geological "uniformitarianism" of James Hutton refuted these theological speculations by demonstrating that geological change was a product of natural forces—wind, rain, and ice—rather than supernatural intervention. Natural landscapes changed through the forces of erosion and upheaval over vast stretches of time, rather than through sudden, cataclysmic destruction. Hutton's concept of a "world machine" envisioned steady, dynamic change throughout the history of the earth. His theory brought stability and predictability to the record of the past that men were beginning to read from rocks and mountains. In doing so, uniformitarianism expanded the geological time scale of the world and inspired confidence in the uniform and predictable workings of nature.

Two other early "time voyagers" who helped to reconstruct the "pirate chart" were William Smith and Baron Georges Cuvier. Smith, an English surveyor and civil engineer, discovered the principle of stratigraphy, by which scientists could identify strata by the fossils found within them, the lowest levels almost always containing the oldest remains. About this same time, Cuvier, "the magician of the charnel house," was working with fossil deposits in the Paris Basin and demonstrating the morphological relationship between extinct vertebrates and living species. Cuvier, who stopped short of endorsing evolution, nevertheless provided the evidence to demonstrate that extinction was a reality and that extinct forms were structurally related to existing creatures. Through these discoveries geology and later biology were able to dispense with supernaturalism and explain the formation and development of the natural world through natural causes. Sir Charles Lyell, in his *Principles of Geology* (1834), was able to offer a comprehensive account of "the world made natural." The stage was now set for the "minor evolutionists" who directly preceded Darwin.

The Making of the *Origin*

One reason that the theory of evolution took so long to emerge is that its proofs are largely inferential. Darwin's theory of descent with modification by natural selection does not lend itself to the same kinds of verification as many of the laws of chemistry or physics. The evidence for the evolution of life is so diverse and complex that Darwinian theory becomes a grand synthesis of information from all the life sciences, along with those related fields—notably geology and paleontology—that account for the physical and natural history of the past. Darwin has repeatedly been accused of a lack of originality, or worse, by critics who could not appreciate the novelty of his theory or would not accept it because it conflicted with their religious or metaphysical beliefs. Despite the fact that the idea of evolution was suggested by several thinkers prior to Darwin—and was perhaps even part of the spirit of the early Victorian period—Darwin was still the first person to amass the wealth of factual detail to demonstrate the mechanisms of organic evolution, through inheritance, variability, competition, natural selection, divergence, and extinction. Darwin and Alfred Russel Wallace, the co-discoverers of natural selection, were practicing naturalists with a wide range of field experiences. The work of their predecessors, however interesting, is for the most part unsupported speculation. The so-called "minor evolutionists"—William Webb, Patrick Matthew, and Robert Chambers—may have suspected that some "law" of organic change operated in the natural world, but they lacked the evidence to demonstrate *how* it worked. The details of natural selection remained for Darwin and Wallace to unfold in their joint papers, which were read before the Linnean Society in July, 1858, and published with the Society's *Journal* that same year.[3]

The middle chapters of Eiseley's book, which review Darwin's accomplishments, are in some respects the least satisfactory part of *Darwin's Century*. The effect of Eiseley's presentation is to minimize Darwin's accomplishment by emphasizing the work of earlier evolutionists. Especially in his discussion of the background of Darwin's thought, Eiseley implicitly questions the originality of Darwin's contribution to biology by stressing the influence of Erasmus Darwin, Lyell, Humboldt, Wallace, and Lamarck. Even in this book Eiseley expresses strong reservations about the influence of Malthus on Darwin's formulation of the principle of natural selection: "it has always seemed dubious to the present writer [Eiseley] that Darwin received his complete inspiration on the selective aspect of the struggle for existence from Malthus, or from his South American observations" (180). This skepticism eventually grew much stronger, after Eiseley discovered the forgotten 1835–37 essays of Edward Blyth, a minor evolutionist. These findings came too late to be incorporated in the text of *Darwin's Century,* but Eiseley considered his discovery so important that he published this information in a separate paper, "Charles Darwin, Edward Blyth, and the Theory of Natural Selection," which appeared the following year in the *Proceedings of the American Philosophical Society.* When Eiseley realized that his essay would not receive an adequate circulation in the *Proceedings,* he decided to expand it into book form, and the posthumously published *Darwin and the Mysterious Mr. X* reflects his fuller treatment of this issue, to which we will return later.

The Challenge to Darwinism

In the last third of *Darwin's Century,* Eiseley traces the series of scientific challenges that ultimately led to advances in evolutionary theory. In a very real sense, the history of Victorian science centers upon the issue of Darwinism. Huxley and other supporters of Darwin may have easily silenced the theological critics, but there subsequently emerged a series of scientific challenges that were not finally resolved until the end of the nineteenth century, and which forced Darwin to retreat from or qualify his original hypothesis and fall back upon a Lamarckian position in later editions of the *Origin.* As Lord Salisbury commented in 1894, there were two strong objections to the Darwinian hypothesis: the insufficiency of time to allow gradual biological change and the impossibility of demonstrating natural selection in detail.

Fleeming Jenkin, a Scotch engineer, raised a major objection to Darwinian theory when he demonstrated in an 1867 paper that it was mathematically impossible for fortuitous variations to become established in a species population, because, given the contemporary assumption of blending inheritance, new variants that arose would soon be swamped out and disappear. Darwin was forced to give up the theory of blending inheritance and fall back on a Lamarckian notion of "pangenesis," which subsequently proved unworkable.

The other major challenge to Darwin was advanced by a physicist, William Thomson, later Lord Kelvin, who disputed the Darwinian assumption of unlimited geological time. By calculating the theoretical rate of dissipation of heat from the earth and the sun, Kelvin arrived at an age of not more than thirty million years for the earth. Disheartened by these objections to his uniformitarian geology, Darwin had to find ways of theoretically demonstrating how natural selection could occur more rapidly in a reduced time scale. In later editions of the *Origin,* he postulated the inheritance of habits or other acquired characteristics that represent a reversion to a basically Lamarckian position. Kelvin's objections were soon to be disproved by discoveries in atomic physics, and in 1900 the rediscovery of the work of Gregor Mendel was to refute the notion of blending inheritance, but by the 1870s, Darwinism was very much on the defensive.

Darwin and Wallace on Human Evolution

The greatest challenge to Darwinism, however, was to formulate an adequate theory of human evolution. This issue was so laden with theological emotion that in the first edition of *The Origin of Species,* Darwin sidestepped the question altogether, remarking cryptically that "light will be thrown on the origin of man and his history." When he finally published *The Descent of Man* in 1871, Darwin still possessed remarkably little direct evidence of man's physical or cultural evolution, so that he was forced to construct his arguments on a series of extensive extrapolations from the operation of natural selection among lower animals. Many of Darwin's hypotheses have since been verified, but the conjectural nature of his views led to the eventual disagreement between Darwin and Wallace over the rate and sequence of human evolution and the problem of explaining the uniqueness of the human brain. Chapter 10, "The Reception of the First Missing Links," which was originally read before the Johns Hopkins History of Ideas Club, and chapter 11, "Wallace and the Human Brain," comprise the most interesting section of *Darwin's Century* because here Eiseley traces the complexities of Victorian thought on the ultimate mystery, the evolution of man, drawing upon his extensive knowledge of the history of anthropological thought.

Eiseley is critical of the Darwinian version of human evolution, since Darwin was a poor ethnologist and did too much theorizing on so little evidence, indulging in the same kind of unsupported speculation of which he disapproved in his grandfather, Erasmus Darwin. Darwin was also misled by the various cultural and racial prejudices of Victorian England in overemphasizing the importance of competition and brute struggle in the course of human evolution, and in viewing non-Caucasian cultures as living examples of man in a primitive or atavistic state, with some evolutionists even placing the Hottentot between European man and the ape. Darwin failed to distinguish between the physical and cultural determinants of human nature, and critics such as the Duke of Argyll soon pointed to inconsistencies in his position. If man's ancestor was a large, gorilloid type of primate with protruding canines and a sagittal crest on his skull, as Darwin originally envisioned, then how could natural selection have favored the evolution of a smaller, physically weaker descendant, if struggle and the "survival of the fittest" were indeed operative? Much of this confusion arose from the absence of an adequate fossil record of early man. Some Darwinians mistook recent human atavisms and "reversions," as well as so-called "primitive" races and cultures, for genuine information about man's ancestry. Another common Victorian misconception was that man had "descended" from the living species of great apes, through a "missing link," rather than sharing with them a common remote ancestor. Lacking any true estimate of human antiquity, nineteenth-century scientists could not even agree whether man was ascending or descending, though they seemed determined to fix a direction to human evolution. As Eiseley demonstrates, few evolutionists could escape the white, ethnocentric bias of the age, which assumed implicitly that Caucasian man stood at the forefront of evolutionary change, while below him were ranked the nonwhite races in descending order from man to ape.

Wallace alone was refreshingly free from these racial and cultural prejudices, perhaps because he had spent more time among the so-called primitive cultures. On the subject of human evolution Wallace disagreed with Darwin on three important issues. While Darwin emphasized variation, competition, and sexual selection as the major forces in the evolution of man, Wallace believed that man had changed little physically in comparison to other Pleistocene fauna, that racial distinctions do not represent successive stages of human evolution, and that with the emergence of the human brain the entire process of natural selection had been altered. Human evolution, Wallace argued, occurred in two successive stages, with the achievement of bipedal posture and the subsequent freeing of the hand to manipulate objects being followed by a different kind of evolutionary change in the rapid increase in the size of the human brain. The first stage of man's evolution involved a change in structure or parts, but the second stage enabled man to evade the trap of specialization by evolving an organ—the brain—that allows him to adapt to changing circumstances without resorting to changes in structure. Man has been able to transfer to his tools and inventions the burden of specialized evolution that limits the rest of the plant and animal world. Wallace introduced the concept of latency—that the human brain had evolved far in excess of its immediate needs, so that the brain of the savage was not inferior to that of the European. Despite his later interest in spiritualism and mysticism (traits that Eiseley has also been accused of showing), Wallace paid closer attention to the available evidence of human evolution and emphasized cultural evolution far more than did Darwin, who refused to acknowledge the transcendent significance of the rise of intelligence on earth. What distressed Darwin and prejudiced other evolutionists against Wallace was his assumption that "some higher intelligence" may have directed human evolution. Eiseley restored Wallace's most significant contributions to the issue of human evolution, while at the same time avoiding his supernaturalism, and stressed the originality of Wallace's speculations about the absolutely unprecedented nature of the human brain, an organ so versatile that it enables man to discover ways of adapting to a constantly changing environment, while he remains physically unchanged—a creature existing both within and outside of nature. Wallace's view of human evolution, in modified form, became an important influence on Eiseley's subsequent thought, as he moved from the history to the philosophy of science in *The Invisible Pyramid* and *The Unexpected Universe*. Here Eiseley presented his own views of man's cultural evolution and his distinctiveness as a creature bound by time and memory—views strongly influenced by Francis Bacon and Alfred Russel Wallace.

The Darwinian Legacy

Given Eiseley's devotion to scholarship and his facility in unraveling the history of ideas, it is regrettable that he became sidetracked by the Darwin-Blyth issue and never completed the sequel to *Darwin's Century*. In his concluding chapter Eiseley recapitulates his major arguments and indicates how much remained to be done in tracing the ramifications of Darwinism in twentieth-century scientific and cultural thought. Even so, the conclusion to *Darwin's Century*, with its focus on time—cyclic, historical, and natural—provides a logical transition to his next book, *The Firmament of Time*, in which Eiseley revised and condensed the major theoretical concepts from his history of evolutionary thought and recast them as a series of meditative essays, without their extensive documentation.

Ideas, Eiseley argued in the conclusion to *Darwin's Century*, evolve, erode, and change over the course of time, in much the same way as the constantly changing surface of the earth. Here he demonstrated that he was not exclusively concerned with the intellectual history of the concept of evolution, but with its impact on man as he gradually responded to the shock of learning that he was part of nature, an animal among animals with a recoverable natural history.

Darwin's century was marked by a changing concept of time, for, in Eiseley's words, "The unique and unreturning nature of the past began early to evince itself." Discoveries in geology, paleontology, astronomy, and physics all pointed to the complete historicity of the world and the constant emergence of novelty. Through the discovery of biological evolution, time became a one-way mirror, "noncyclic, unreturning, and creative." But in this mirror man saw himself as more of a beast than an angel:

Caliban had supplanted Ariel. In their zealousness for this new view of man, Victorian evolutionists may well have overemphasized culturally relative concepts of competition and struggle, and ignored the basic inner stability of organisms and the long-term continuity of life. Although in the newly opened book of time the Victorians read only of struggle, competition, and extinction, there is far more to the evolutionary story than this. The "law of succession of types" that Darwin formulated was a morphological principle—an expression of the relationship between living and dead forms—as well as a way of accounting for extinction. Examples of altruism and cooperation occur in nature just as often as brute struggle and "the survival of the fittest," as Eiseley reminds us.

This balanced view of evolutionary change has great import for our understanding of human culture. The nineteenth century might justify slavery and imperialism through the use of a pernicious social Darwinism, but these qualities were less intrinsic to human nature than a reflection of the Victorian outlook. To accept these views today by rationalizing social ills as products of our inherited and unbendable "human nature" is dangerously to circumscribe the range of human possibilities. It is to deny our potential freedom to become what we desire—or imagine—ourselves to be.

Despite its formidable topic, this otherwise scholarly book ends on a curiously visionary note, more typical of Eiseley's writing elsewhere. Eiseley returns to Wallace's views of the human brain as a unique "organ of indeterminism" in nature, freeing us from the bonds of specialization, but substituting instead a terrible burden of choice in forcing us to determine who and what we shall be—individually and as a species. Eiseley rejects the implications of Darwinian determinism and insists instead that man is "protean," a fully volitional creature capable of shaping his own fate from the world within his mind—the world of dream, memory, and culture— and imposing that vision upon external nature. *Darwin's Century* concludes with a personal anecdote: the story of a Mexican peon and his wife who welcomed the writer with innate dignity and generosity when he wandered lost and exhausted into their camp. Such men of "simple culture" are not "moral fossils" but representatives of man transcending the instinctive selfishness of the natural order through recourse to his inner world of altruistic impulses and ideals. Eiseley's final praise and respect are granted not to the materialistic or mechanistic aspects of Darwin's legacy, but to the vision of human betterment, extending across cultural boundaries, that this simple Mexican shares with the Victorian Darwin—not Darwin the scientist but Darwin the visionary naturalist who was able to express in his 1837 notebook a comprehensive and humane view of life, human and animal, "all melted together."

The Firmament of Time

The favorable reception of *The Immense Journey* and *Darwin's Century* made Eiseley a respected interpreter of science by the early 1960s and his reputation launched him into a hectic series of lectures, speeches, and public appearances. With the American interest in science intensified after the Sputnik scare, public engagements kept him busy, and if he lectured and traveled too much, he relished the prestige and honor. Eiseley was an impressive lecturer, with a deep, resonant voice and a sense of the histrionic. His desire to "perform" was perhaps inherited from his father, an unsuccessful actor, so that his public lectures may have been a way of fulfilling his father's unrealized dreams. The lectures, along with magazine articles, also served as a forum in which he could try out new ideas before they found their way into his books.

In the fall of 1959 Eiseley accepted an invitation to deliver six lectures as visiting professor of the philosophy of science at the University of Cincinnati College of Medicine. The series, originally entitled "Man's Quest for Certainty," was sponsored by the Markle Foundation through a grant to the Department of Physiology. The purpose of the lectureship was to promote "a better understanding of the role of science as its own evolution permeates and controls the thought of men through the centuries." Well-received, his lectures were published as *The Firmament of Time* (1960), which won the John Burroughs Medal for the best publication in the field of nature writing, and the Lecomte du Nouy Foundation Award for "best work of particular interest for the spiritual life of our epoch and for the defense of human dignity." It was also a runner-up in the nonfiction category of the National Book Awards for 1960.

The Firmament of Time is deceptively short and simple. Eiseley explains how man came to accept the earth, death, life, and human existence as "natural" (part of the natural order) rather than "supernatural" (part of a divinely ordained plan or design). The first four chapters are in one sense an extended meditation on the meaning of the word "natural," a concept notoriously difficult to define. What, after all, is "natural"? Eiseley's essays provide a lucid, imaginative account of the emergence of the modern scientific world view during the past three centuries. "The firmament of time," a phrase borrowed from stanza 44 of Shelley's "Adonais," Eiseley applies to time made natural. The last dimension to be mastered by man, it has been penetrated through the reconstruction of geological history and evolutionary change. Eiseley uses the phrase to suggest the paradox inherent in man's mastery of an inscrutable dimension, at once palpable and elusive. Though "firmament" comes from a Latin term meaning strong support or prop to hold things up, its primary meaning is the vault of heaven, or the sky, in the Ptolemaic sense of that outermost, fixed sphere of the heavens in which the stars were located. A "firmament of time" may be said to exist metaphorically in the geological and fossil record of the earth, through which the natural history of life may be read by the knowledgeable observer. Though to interpret that record correctly is to make every event on this planet "natural," it is not necessarily to diminish its importance. Reduction has been the thrust of Western science, but "life was not made natural in a day, nor in a single generation," Eiseley reminds us.

Four Meditations on "Natural"

In *The Firmament of Time* Eiseley reworked his chronological presentation of the sequence of discoveries and ideas that led up to Darwin's theory of evolution and gave rise to a series of concise thematic arguments. If *Darwin's Century* is essentially an historical treatment of evolution, then *The Firmament of Time* is lyrical and meditative. If the first study concentrates on the history of science, its sequel expresses the poetry of science: the beauty and elegance, as well as the explanatory power, of a master hypothesis that irrevocably altered our world view. Thus the first four chapters of *The Firmament* are condensed from various sections of *Darwin's Century,* and the last two chapters, on the "humanness" of man and the "naturalness" of nature, anticipate subsequent books. Since the six lectures were originally intended to be heard, not read, Eiseley concentrates on evoking the arresting image, the eloquent phrase or turn of thought. The originality of *The Firmament* exploits Eiseley's gift for the imaginative. It shows once again that Eiseley was poetically rather than philosophically minded, that his best essays are personal musings rather than systematic works of philosophy.

His treatment of time, for instance, primarily discusses the impact of geological and biological chronology on the human imagination. It never attempts rigorously to distinguish among various philosophical definitions of time. Eiseley's "time made natural" limns an intellectual comprehension of the vast reaches of time as they affect our subjective experience on a human scale. To explore the concept of time in greater depth he would have needed the conceptual skill of a Bergson, Whitehead, or Popper, but Eiseley never pretended to be an analytical philosopher of science. His intuitions were more akin to those of Pascal than those of Descartes. Because his primary concern throughout is humanistic, time made natural never becomes mechanistic or deterministic for him, even though he fully accepts the transition from a god-centered to a man-centered view of the world, which historically accompanied this extension of time. Finally, the vast framework of natural time, Eiseley argues, has wrought a change in modern human consciousness as drastic as that which the Copernican and Galilean extensions of the cosmos wrought upon the Renaissance mind. It has met with as much resistance, since man is basically a romantic (and an egotist) about his place in the world. In this adjustment of scale, man has applied both his pragmatic and mystical impulses to comprehend his diminished place in an expanded, naturalized world. Thus man's perception of time has evolved culturally from the timeless present of primitive man to the rhythms and cycles of the sun cultures, then to the nonreturning, linear time of Judeo-Christian belief, and at last to the newest scientific time and relativity.

Each chapter of *The Firmament of Time* introduces a key conceptual innovation that "naturalized" the past. Thus chapter 1, "How the World Became Natural," explores advances in eighteenth-century geology, particularly in the thought of James Hutton, the founder of historical geology. Through the work of men like Hutton, changes in the surface of the earth were for the first time brought under the domain of natural law rather than myth and superstition. With Hutton, who knew how to read the passage of time from the rocks and who could read the fate of mountains in moving streams, man first learned the true age of the earth. Though Hutton understood the mechanics of geological change, he could not decide among his analogies whether the earth was a machine or an organism—whether its laws were fixed or dynamic.

In chapter 2, "How Death Became Natural," Eiseley discusses the disturbing issue of extinction—the disappearance of entire species—a fact long denied by the orthodox mind because of the belief that a providential God would not permit such waste or loss of life. Men reacted with horror to the evidence of extinction read from fossil remains because they reasoned that if any species could disappear, then none were assured permanence, including man himself. Religious commentators invented elaborate explanations to account for extinction within a biblical context, including the short-lived theory of catastrophism, with its violent cataclysms and successive creations, which made extinction theologically acceptable.

Then Charles Lyell, in his *Principles of Geology,* demonstrated how long-term geological change was bound to affect the course of life on earth. He showed that the world remains in dynamic, rather than static balance. At that point, man was on the verge of discovering that life, as well as time, was linear, historical, and unrepeatable.

Chapter 3, "How Life Became Natural," briefly rehearses the story of the discovery of biological evolution. Since it summarizes Eiseley's major arguments about Darwin's forerunners, it is a chapter useful to read before beginning *Darwin's Century.* Using an orchestral analogy, Eiseley suggests that all the separate parts of evolutionary theory were ready to be harmonized when, in 1859, Darwin stepped up to the podium to conduct the performance. To support this revisionist position, Eiseley introduces the Coleridgean theory of creativity later expanded in the essay, "Darwin, Coleridge, and the Theory of Unconscious Creation," which appeared in *Darwin and the Mysterious Mr. X.* In an essentially romantic theory of creativity, Eiseley follows Coleridge's lead in arguing that the great geniuses of any era have a facility for plucking out ideas hovering in the intellectual climate of an era, ready to be expressed. This version of Darwin's accomplishment, however, places too much emphasis on theorizing and gives too little weight to the enormous mass of empirical evidence Darwin accumulated. Darwin also made two crucial additions to the incomplete ideas of his predecessors: he saw natural selection as a creative rather than a restrictive force, not merely maintaining the fixity of species but creating new ones; and he proposed "natural selection without balance" as a continuous force in nature, working through random and accidental variations. The chapter ends with a vivid Eiseley anecdote to illustrate his theme: since man is "natural," why should he predominate? Eiseley tells how he was once locked in a natural history museum overnight, in a hall with the Crustacea. Reflecting the sunset through the display cases, their exoskeletons reminded him of the incredible potentialities inherent in any single form. Nevertheless, he was glad to meet another vertebrate in the form of the museum guard. The orders of life are like multifaceted diamonds with their countless glittering surfaces, he reflects, and man constitutes but one pattern—one reflection—amid the uncountable multiplicity of life.

Chapter 4, "How Man Became Natural," reviews the major paleoanthropological discoveries that allowed man gradually to reconstruct his evolutionary past. It focuses on the debate about whether man is "innately" aggressive or altruistic. Here Eiseley briefly sketches his own views of human nature—based more on the approach of Wallace than that of

Darwin. Eiseley insists upon the determining influence of custom and culture in the humanization of man without suggesting, as some anthropologists have done, that man's tool-making and other cultural proclivities somehow preceded the development of his intellect. The current biological approach to human evolution seems to imply that man's simple tool-making and social instincts gradually selected for greater intelligence, which would obviously be important for any social creature. Yet Wallace and Eiseley argue conversely that the sudden and dramatic increase in man's brain and his subsequent cultural advances—in language, thought, learning, and social behavior—cannot be entirely explained by natural processes. Our cultural evolution has now superseded our physical evolution as the primary force in the shaping of our human nature, and Eiseley warns that, as contemporary man loses touch with the restraining hand of custom and culture, he gradually loses his humanity.

The chapter begins with an anecdote about a barren and desolate landscape of glacial boulders in northeastern Nebraska, a glacial moraine that reminds Eiseley how important was the last ice age as the environment in which man became recognizably human. Glaciers, not floods, were the cataclysms that primitive man experienced, as he retreated before the advance of the ice across the face of Europe and Asia. A hundred years ago, the discovery of the first Neanderthal remains prompted a debate over the "nature" of primitive man—was he a savage beast or a sociable primate? In an imaginative reconstruction of social life among the Neanderthals, Eiseley shows that this dichotomy is a false one, since evidence from burial caves and campsites, such as the offerings placed with the dead, suggest that distinctly human cultural traits were evident quite early in man's development. Eiseley particularly objects to the Dart-Lorenz position that emphasizes man's "innate" aggressiveness as a primate who evolved without the inhibiting mechanisms to prevent him from killing his own kind, once his tool and weapon-making abilities transformed him into a hunter. In other words, some ethologists believe that murder and homicide are part of our biological heritage—that brute nature we carry within ourselves. For some reason our moral inhibitions simply have not kept pace with our weapons-producing ability. Eiseley cites Dr. L. S. B. Leakey's work in the Olduvai Gorge to oppose this grim conclusion and to insist upon the social and altruistic qualities of primitive man. Still, even though man has become natural, "the nature of his 'naturalness' escapes him," because, for Eiseley, human nature is at least partially a matter of human choice, since man has some power in defining his own "second nature," his cultural evolution.

The Two "Natures" of Man

After chapter 4, the focus of the book shifts to the future, as Eiseley examines man's prospects in a change-oriented society, indifferent to humane culture, the historical past, or nature. The future he contemplates is at best ambiguous. Man is wrestling with a projection of himself disguised as the future, and, as Kierkegaard warns, "he who fights the future has a dangerous enemy." The last two chapters of *The Firmament of Time* are the most speculative and intellectually exciting, though stylistically uneven, as Eiseley combines his scientific and humanistic insights in a set of prophecies about the dangers of narrowing human nature to a "single vision." Eiseley's practice of adapting essays originally written on separate topics and including them in a single book contributes to the unevenness of style in chapter 5. Some of the passages here are too rhetorical or overdrawn, reflecting the context for which the essay was originally written, as part of a collection on "social control in a free society."[4]

In chapter 5, "How Human is Man?", Eiseley demonstrates how the success of the scientific revolution has resulted in a new, diminished view of human nature. Man has plumbed the dimension of time and reanimated the stage on which the play of life has been enacted, though he now fears that he may not be the leading actor in the pageant. In contemplating an increasingly ominous future, man is beginning to realize that his greatest danger is not external nature but himself—"man made natural." With the coming of *Homo sapiens,* a vast hole has been opened in the instinctual order of nature, threatening to engulf the natural world in a whirlpool of destructive energy. The human brain has emancipated man from the restraints of instinct governing other forms of life, yet since man craves stability, human culture has become a substitute for these instinctual restraints. As Francis Bacon suggested, human culture is a "second nature" that man raises from within himself, so that art and nature ought to be complementary forces. Yet one dimension of that cultural order, our drive to dominate and subdue nature through the use of science and technology, now threatens to destroy the balance of both the natural order and our entire cultural heritage by unleashing powers beyond man's capacity to control. Contemporary man now fears that he may not have a future to enjoy, that Bacon's dream of attaining a "secular paradise" through the powers of science may have turned into an uncontrollable nightmare.

Eiseley envisions a new man now emerging, an "asphalt man" estranged from nature and lacking pity or compassion toward any form of life. He cites a remark made to him by a young man as an example of this new barbarism: "'Why can't we just eventually kill off everything and live here by ourselves with more room? We'll be able to synthesize food pretty soon.'" Nor is this attitude limited to a few, since it in fact reflects the hubris of our age, which perceives man as separate and independent from nature, able to subsist entirely through his own technological ingenuity. Eiseley notes three dangers inherent in this view: the rapidity of change does not allow our culture time to adjust, so that we are swept away by the tide of events; men no longer have the time and leisure for reflection; and as a consequence, a new, one-dimensional man has emerged, who exercises power without responsibility, and who has almost succeeded in transforming himself into a machine. The mass loss of a personal ethic in favor of a group ethic heightens the dangers of our secular conception of progress. Without an inward ethic of restraint we will lose our cultural stability. Eiseley uses two metaphors to depict these opposing forces of chaos and order: the whirlpool (or maelstrom) and the spider web. The "torrent" evokes an image of technological forces accelerating out of control, of unrestricted chaos, which is opposed by the "web" of cultural continuity, of mutual compassion and ethical responsibility for all forms of life. The chapter then concludes with a set of contrasting parables about two opposing "types" of modern man—an alcoholic derelict who denies responsibility for his condition ("I'm an alcoholic. I can't help myself") and pleads for a handout, and a compassionate physicist, who refuses even to remove a small tortoise from its place in the woods because he has "'tampered enough with the universe.'" The choice of moral evasion or ethical responsibility—denying or affirming ourselves and our kinship with the rest of life—will, in Eiseley's final analysis, be the measure of the humanness of man.

The last chapter, originally entitled "Nature, Man, and Miracles," was later recast as "How Natural is 'Natural'?"[5] In this most literary and speculative part of *The Firmament of Time,* Eiseley inquires whether we may properly call anything in the external world "natural," since the very perspective we apply comes from within us. Ironically, we are life become conscious of itself, now divorcing itself from the rest of life, using an outmoded distinction between man and the rest of the world: between art (or the artificial) and nature. The apparent "naturalness" of life is the product of our scientific imagination, which seeks to impose order and regularity on the "chaos" that we do not yet understand. For the empirical mind, the act of understanding implies a reduction, because naming, ordering, and explaining natural phenomena strip them of their mystery and awe; man assumes that naming (or comprehending) implies mastering, and thus tangible nature is reduced to an abstract theory or hypothesis. Eiseley strongly objects to this imagined act of power and control over nature, which is more illusive than real, and suggests instead a relationship of empathy and compassion. Science, he reminds us, may abstract its theories from reality, but does not have the power to dominate or control it.

The extreme of this "rational" irrationality appears in the case of the paranoid scientist, an apocryphal character who in his declining years wore heavy rubber boots to keep from falling through the "interstices" of molecular space. A victim of his own theory or view of the natural world—admittedly a bizarre one—he illustrates how unquestioned "scientific" theory has the power to warp and destroy.

Contrasted with the irrational, solipsistic world of the eccentric physicist is the Edenic world of a young muskrat that Eiseley spots beneath a boat dock on a New England lake. Too young to have learned to fear man, the creature is unaware of his danger until Eiseley drops several pebbles in the water nearby to warn him away. Having instructed the muskrat about the "nature" of the world that he shares with man, Eiseley walks away, "pleased that darkness had not gained on life by any act of mine."

By "nature," Eiseley suggests that we often mean the mechanistic secondary laws which regulate the natural world. But if nature is governed by such laws, then miracles, or interruptions in their operation, are "God's Prerogative." The reductionistic sense of "natural" implies that all natural events are predictable, and thus it fails to allow for the possibility of randomness or change. This eighteenth-century view of nature, which is still to a great extent with us, is completely at odds with the major discoveries in twentieth-century physics and astronomy that have restored openness to the world under the names of relativity and indeterminacy. At the most elemental levels of matter and energy, we do not find a world rigidly governed by natural law but an open universe, subject to infinite possibilities and contingencies. Thus the conventional view of nature is at odds with recent theoretical discoveries in science in a kind of "cultural lag" in assimilating the thought of Einstein, Heisenberg, and other modern physicists. Nor will even the most up-to-date knowledge by itself bring wisdom or compassion until we cure ourselves of what Jacob Bronowski calls "the itch for absolute knowledge and power."

The balance of the final chapter shifts to a series of personal anecdotes, through which Eiseley conveys his vision of a compassionate and humane science. The next incident he describes takes place once again in the Nebraska Badlands, during an archeological expedition. Eiseley relates a quest that began in a mood of weariness and futility, as he rode out of camp on horseback overnight into the nearby mountains. His physical excursion over the dry and broken hills gradually becomes a metaphoric journey back in time, as he descends, stratum by stratum, into the remote geological past. At the end of his figurative descent down the ladder of life, gripped in a mood of depression and emptiness, Eiseley experiences his vision. In a moment of Bergsonian insight, he realizes that flowing through the mind alone is a "stream of consciousness" resisting the current of life that runs from nothingness toward oblivion. Freed from the flow of time, the mind alone can act as a "microcosm" to record and retain the greater world beyond itself. This ability sets man apart from the rest of nature.

At this point the significance of the title and central metaphor of *The Firmament of Time* becomes most explicit. Eiseley resists the temptation to skeptical empiricism—"the black cloud of merciless thought"—and reaffirms that the human mind can indeed transcend "the firmament of time" and recall the past or imagine the future. Still in the grip of the mood evoked by the barren landscape, Eiseley gives way to his visions, as, in a Dickensian moment, he views past, ghostly images of himself as a child and a young man, reviewing the actions that shaped his character, for good or ill. This visionary experience gradually expands into one of intellectual daring—imagining "divine relativity" in an imperfect cosmos—as Eiseley speculates, "perhaps God himself may rove in similar pain up the dark roads of his universe." He implies that God may be limited in his omnipotence—though not in his love and compassion—and that man is in a sense self-created through his intellect and imagination. Man "creates" himself through the discovery of his evolutionary past. To dramatize this point, Eiseley imaginatively recapitulates phylogeny as he reconstructs man's evolutionary history toward the present moment.

This remarkable passage echoes both the conventions of the Native American shamanistic experience and the "descent motif" in classical and medieval literature, where the protagonist ventures into the underworld to discover some truth about himself—and more broadly about his culture's past and future prospects—and ultimately returns with a saving vision. As Eiseley had remarked earlier in "The Judgment of the Birds," this is the function of the literary naturalist in the modern world: to bring back "a natural revelation." But as Eiseley also confesses, there is a price to be paid for such insight, not only in solitude. His imagination is haunted by time, by a sense of perpetual strangeness, and by his sense of having seen the "crack into the Absolute."

Nature, rather than being mundane and predictable, is for Eiseley "one vast miracle transcending the reality of night and nothingness." Like the mythical tree of Igdrasil, it perpetually emerges "out of darkness towards the light." We live on the verge of the miraculous, at the point where the miraculous comes into being, and after it has appeared we call it "natural." Nor is it wise to take nature for granted, for, as Santayana warned, "nature is filled with coiled springs." Eiseley increasingly believed that man's role is to cherish and protect that miraculous element in life, as in the case of another Badlands incident, or "natural revelation," he witnessed involving a black snake and a hen pheasant. In this remarkable natural epiphany Eiseley came across a death struggle involving the two creatures, and each was unable to escape from the other until he freed the bird from the serpent's coils, arbitrating between both lives in that desperate confrontation of scales and feathers. His act of compassion leads to a more comprehensive vision of himself.

The Firmament of Time ends with what can only be described as a highly unusual affirmation of faith on the part of an unconventional believer— whom some have called a "midnight optimist" or a "Christian agnostic." Perhaps the distance between skepticism and belief has grown smaller in our age, or else he is simply affirming that the heart of science is a mystery, a great unknowable, but he articulates an act of faith in a comprehensive vision of life that transcends reductionistic science and celebrates the birth of a new self in touch with the Infinite, a belief in a new compassionate ethic linking all forms of life in a vast web of being. Eiseley finally denies the "naturalness" of the earth, death, life, and man because, as Pascal said, "what we make natural we destroy." In a world of constantly emerging novelty, of radical contingency and indeterminacy, nothing can be merely "natural," especially man. "Man made natural" is man predictable, fatalistic, deterministic—controlled by environment, society, or genes—with no freedom of choice, no free will, no possibility of transcendence.

His faith in the future also leads him to oppose those forces in science that have caused a narrowing of human knowledge or a diminishment of man. He raises precisely those humanistic questions of quality and value that positivists dismiss as methodologically unanswerable and hence irrelevant. Without such reflection, he warns, we will be engulfed in the "whirlpool" of rapidly accumulating scientific knowledge and accelerating change: we will become victims of knowledge and power without a human face. Science need not and should not be wed to a "naturalistic" world view, he concludes, and the morality of science must move beyond the calculation of probabilities to the area of humane choice.

Darwin and the Mysterious Mr. X.

The forgotten papers of Edward Blyth, which Eiseley discovered when he began his research for the sequel to *Darwin's Century,* continued to haunt his imagination even after he put aside his plans to write a second volume of his history of Darwinism. Though he subsequently published "Charles Darwin, Edward Blyth, and the Theory of Natural Section" with the *Proceedings of the American Philosophical Society* in 1959, he still felt that his findings deserved wider publicity. So Eiseley planned a book-length collection of essays on the Darwin-Blyth issue to restate his case, a project left unfinished at his death in 1977, and finally completed two years later by his editor, Kenneth Heuer. Yet there is some question whether *Darwin and the Mysterious Mr. X* represents Eiseley's final intentions. Even the title of the book was taken from a working manuscript and probably would not have been Eiseley's final choice. One wonders about the rationale for bringing these previously published essays together in book form without adding any substantially new evidence to Eiseley's original argument, particularly in light of recent Darwin scholarship.[6]

Darwin and the Mysterious Mr. X: New Light on the Evolutionists is a miscellaneous collection of eight Eiseley essays first published between 1959 and 1972, along with documentation concerning Edward Blyth. Part 1, "The Dancers in the Ring," is introduced by three short essays on Darwin, Wallace, and Lyell, followed by the two keynote essays, "Charles Darwin, Edward Blyth, and the Theory of Natural Selection," and "Darwin, Coleridge, and the Theory of Unconscious Creation," which present Eiseley's case for Blyth and explore Darwin's ostensible reasons for failing to mention him. Part 2, "The Documentary Evidence," contains reprints of the three original Blyth articles, "The Varieties of Animals," "Seasonal and Other Changes in Birds," and "Psychological Distinctions Between Man and Other Animals," all published in the *Magazine of Natural History* between 1835 and 1837. Part 3, "The Forgotten Parent," contains a short biographical sketch of Edward Blyth written by his friend Arthur Grote for the *Journal of the Asiatic Society of Bengal* in 1875. Part 4, "The Evolution of Man," includes three of Eiseley's essays unrelated to the Blyth issue: "Neanderthal Man and the Dawn of Human Paleontology," "The Intellectual Antecedents of *The Descent of Man,*" and "The Time of Man."

As his main thesis, Eiseley proposes that Darwin failed to acknowledge his use of Blyth's work, particularly the three 1835–37 essays, in formulating his theory of natural selection. According to Eiseley, Darwin returned home from his five-year voyage on the *Beagle* convinced of the reality of evolution but still unable to account for its mechanics in nature. The solution to his problem came not from reading Malthus, as Darwin later claimed, but from his careful study of Blyth's three articles in the *Magazine of Natural History,* which were published during this time. Later Darwin allegedly concealed the original source of his ideas and followed Wallace's lead in substituting mention of Malthus's population studies instead. Eiseley bases his conjectures largely on Darwin's chance use of a rare term, "inosculate," in his 1836 notebook—a term that Blyth had previously used in his articles—and on Darwin's incorporating into the *Origin* and subsequent works Blyth's arguments on mutative types in domestication, hybridity, protective coloration, the homing instinct in animals, and the instinctive shamming of death. Darwin then supposedly removed sections of his 1837 notebook to hide his intellectual trail back to his original sources. Yet scholars who have reconstructed Darwin's notebooks recently and found these "lost" pages indicate that he simply cut out the useful pages from his bound notebooks and refiled them by category, a technique that he also used with some of the books in his library to facilitate his reading.[7]

Eiseley's quarrel seems to be primarily with Darwin's failure to acknowledge Blyth's influence—if it was such—in the first and subsequent editions of the *Origin,* particularly in the third edition of 1861, which contained an historical introduction to the idea of evolution. He also intimates that Darwin's guilt over this concealment was one of the reasons for his long delay in publishing the *Origin,* a hesitation better explained by Darwin's fears about the intellectual climate in England during this time and his almost neurotic scrupulousness about fact and accuracy in compiling evidence for what he hoped would be a comprehensive work on the "species question." To make his case, Eiseley proceeds via an elaborate analogy between the creative imaginations of Darwin and Samuel Taylor Coleridge, showing how in each case the romantic theory of "unconscious creation" was a polite way of avoiding the difficult issue of potential plagiarism. But the comparison between poetic and scientific creativity has limited application here, and Eiseley soon encounters additional problems. He admits that despite Blyth's long correspondence with Darwin, Blyth may never have recognized his own contribution to evolutionary theory, or even the connection between his own articles and the *Origin,* because he continued to believe in the fixity of species.

Although Eiseley's original essay on Blyth raised some important questions and served as a stimulus to Darwin scholarship, *Darwin and the Mysterious Mr. X* is in many ways his least successful book. Part of the problem rests with its disunified format, but the major flaws seem to be in its outdated scholarship after twenty years and in the tenuous logic of Eiseley's arguments.

Eiseley's Quarrel With Darwin

One senses that Eiseley felt a deep ambivalence toward Darwin, not only for Darwin's literalness and materialistic outlook and for the gradual loss of his taste for poetry and the arts that he confesses in his *Autobiography,* but also for his eminence in the world of science and for the influence that he has exerted in steering modern biology away from a contemplative and toward a strictly empirical study of nature. In several of his books Eiseley refers to Darwin as a "psychological father figure," whose influence has distorted the judgment of modern biologists, especially those unacquainted with the history of ideas. He objects to the "solitary grandeur" in which Darwin is held as the discoverer of evolutionary theory, a thesis implicit throughout *Darwin's Century.* But it was finally with the limitations of Darwin's strict empiricism and his lack of historical insight that Eiseley felt his deepest quarrel, because this approach did not allow room for the older tradition of contemplative natural history, toward which Eiseley felt increasingly drawn—the tradition of "parson-naturalists" that made Darwin's work possible.

Even in *Darwin's Century,* Eiseley's attitude toward Darwin appears sharply ambivalent. Though recognizing the intellectual importance of the *Origin,* both in biological science and other disciplines, he seems unwilling to grant Darwin full credit for the originality of his thought. This critical attitude toward Darwin grew more pronounced with time, as Eiseley sensed a skepticism in academic circles about the implications for Darwin scholarship of his discovery of the Blyth papers. Whether Darwin consciously borrowed from Blyth raises difficult questions of intention and motivation on Darwin's part, if these allegations can be proved. Eiseley implied that Darwin exaggerated his debt to Malthus in order to disguise his actual source in Blyth. Although this matter is still controversial, Eiseley felt that his discovery of the Edward Blyth papers was his major contribution to the history of science. The current thinking among biological historians, however, is that Darwin adequately documented his borrowings from Blyth, and that in any case Eiseley's conviction of Blyth's influence is overstated, since Blyth, along with the other pre-Darwinian evolutionists, saw natural selection as a purely conservative rather than as a creative force.[8]

Yet in other places Eiseley could write about Darwin with great admiration and respect. The story of Eiseley's disenchantment with Darwin is not complete without this balanced perspective, found in an early essay, "The Program on the Darwin Collection in the Library," written for the American Philosophical Society in 1954. In his conclusion to this piece, Eiseley offers this tribute to Darwin, which stands in marked contrast to his later opinions:

One final thing strikes the thoughtful observer as he pores over Darwin's letters, whether published or unpublished. They are rich in a way that no modern scholar of my acquaintance has the time to be rich in his correspondence. They represent the long, thoughtful outpourings of a solitary man in the winter evenings at Down. They range across the world and back, they probe the past, they deal with Providence and those mysteries beneath the basic fabric of the universe. They are also very patient letters for so nervous and distraught a man. They are full of the grave gentleness which is so often lacking in the hysteria of the modern world, and they will stand for all time representative of a day that is gone. A day when men returned to the quiet of a house without radio or television, and found within themselves such treasures to be communicated, as would, long after their deaths, fill volumes and talk attentively to troubled men one hundred years away—men, who, if they stop spinning the fretful dials in the living room, too often feel only the rising of an empty silence in their hearts.[9]

Not only is this passage representative of Eiseley's prose style at its most eloquent and profound, but the tribute that he presents to Darwin might as easily apply to Eiseley himself, alike in his habits of reflection, in his extensive and gracious correspondence, in the qualities of temperament that he reveals in his finest works, and in his place in the world of letters. These same meditative qualities would continue to appear in Eiseley's poetry and prose during the last two decades of his career.

Chapter Four
The Baconian Vision

"The teacher is a sculptor of the intangible future," Eiseley remarked in *The Night Country,* and he never lost his passionate belief in the value of education, particularly for the gifted or talented child from a deprived background, such as his own. A popular professor at the University of Pennsylvania, for twelve years he taught both undergraduate and graduate courses in general anthropology, introduction to archeology, human paleontology, and a variety of graduate seminars, before he was named provost in 1959. Nor did Eiseley neglect his teaching responsibilities during these busy years of scholarship and administrative work. After he resigned as provost in 1961, President Gaylord Harnwell named him first University Professor of Anthropology and the History of Science. Eiseley's appointment began a series of university-wide distinguished professorships at Pennsylvania, later called Benjamin Franklin Professorships, to encourage outstanding faculty members to extend their interests beyond their fields of specialization. The appointment largely freed Eiseley from ordinary departmental responsibilities; he taught one or two interdisciplinary courses per year and devoted the remainder of his time to writing. With his new academic freedom, Eiseley even joined with a colleague from the English Department in planning a graduate seminar in Victorian literature, though the course was never taught. At the same time President Harnwell announced the formation of a Department of the Philosophy and History of Science, to be headed by Eiseley. Since he was then a fellow at the Center for Advanced Study in the Behavioral Sciences at Stanford, Eiseley would assume his new position when he returned to Pennsylvania the following year.

Although Eiseley tended to withdraw from departmental affairs after he was named provost, he maintained his social contacts elsewhere in Philadelphia, including his memberships in the Wistar Association, a group of American Philosophical Society members who met periodically for evenings of good conversation, and the Franklin Inn Club, whose members gathered for weekly dining and literary discussions. Founded by the great Philadelphia neurologist S. Weir Mitchell, who also wrote novels, the Franklin Inn had numbered among its members Owen Wister and Christopher Morley. As Eiseley grew older, such club associations became more important to him as a means to cultivate friendships in comfortable, congenial circumstances with a variety of scientific, literary, and professional men. That was especially important in Philadelphia, which still judges prominent figures according to how "clubbable" they are. One of Eiseley's sketches, "The Dance of the Frogs," in *The Star Thrower,* doubtless takes its inspiration and setting—the Philadelphia Explorers Club—from Eiseley's club experiences.

Otherwise the Eiseleys lived quietly in a large, old-fashioned garden apartment in suburban Wynnewood, along the Philadelphia "Main Line," and limited their circle to a few close friends. As his private book collection grew, they rented the adjoining apartment in their English tudor-style building and converted it into a combination library and study. They remained in Wynnewood Apartments from 1949 onward, and Loren's only real disappointment was that tenants were not allowed to keep pets, although one Christmas the Eiseleys temporarily sheltered a stray kitten named "Night Country."

Eiseley did much of his writing at home, although his insomnia, which grew worse with age, forced him to work at odd hours. Since he did not sleep well he would often get out of bed during the night to make notes or to write. Sometimes he would write through the night and catnap during the day on a couch in his study. His favorite place to write, though, was the dining-room table, where he would compose in longhand and leave the drafts for his wife or his secretary, Caroline Werkley, to type and edit. He was a fitful rather than a steady writer, given to spells of feverish writing, when he would say, "I feel as if I want to write with both hands." Then he might suddenly experience "writer's block" and have to leave a passage temporarily unfinished.

During such interruptions, Eiseley would often put aside his writing and go out walking to visit a friend. A close friend was his fellow Nebraskan author Wright Morris, who until 1958 taught at several colleges in the Philadelphia area, including Haverford and Swarthmore. Morris and his wife lived in Haverford, close to Eiseley's apartment in Wynnewood. Eiseley would often appear unexpectedly at the door, and the two men would chat about some nonliterary topic for diversion, haranguing each other about the foul state of the world or speculating about the Starkweather murders in Lincoln, though on occasion they also talked about literature or about work in progress. Sometimes they amused themselves by watching the local dancing chipmunk, which Morris described in *The Huge Season;* or they might take long walks across the open fields, which later became shopping centers in the Philadelphia suburbs. Morris, who shared more with Eiseley than a Nebraska boyhood—a fascination with time and the tug of memory, apparent in his *World in the Attic* and *The Man Who Was There,* which mirrored much in Eiseley's own life—later dedicated to him *The Works of Love.* Yet even Morris, as a close friend and confidant, found Eiseley by nature reserved and hesitant to reveal what he considered private.

As time reduced the number of Eiseley's friendships in Philadelphia, especially after Wright Morris moved to California, Eiseley built another set of epistolary acquaintances through his books and public appearances. Letters came to him from animal lovers, aspiring writers, would-be biographers, sculptors and artists, psychoanalysts, fellow scientists, even from the translator of one of his books, in Calcutta, requesting help in educating his daughter in America. Most of the mail, however, came from ordinary readers who had queries about his writings. Yet Eiseley tried to answer as many letters as possible, with the help of his secretary, Mrs. Caroline Werkley, dictating full replies. Often he would worry about a problem raised in a letter, as in the case of an eighty-year-old man, who wrote a letter of appreciation explaining that he lived "far from civilization" with only a horse, a dog, and Eiseley's books for companions.[1] Loren wondered what would become of the horse and the dog if anything happened to the old man.

One such friendship developed with Mae Woods Bell, director of the North Carolina Children's Museum in Rocky Mount, after she wrote to Eiseley asking him to inscribe a copy of *The Firmament of Time* for her godchild. Discovering that they shared interests in natural history and museum work, they continued to exchange letters, and Eiseley often visited her during his speaking tours through the Southeast. In appreciation for her kindness, he later dedicated to her the poem "Safe in the Toy Box," found in *Another Kind of Autumn,* knowing that she would understand his metaphor of museums as "time machines," with glass display cases, or "toy boxes," providing safe repositories for the pharoah's artifacts, designed "to hold time as it was."

The Man Who Saw Through Time

Had Eiseley needed a role model for his career after the publication of *The Immense Journey* in 1957, it would clearly have been Sir Francis

Bacon—diplomat, jurist, administrator, author, philosopher, "time traveler," and prophet of science—rather than the reclusive Charles Darwin. Eiseley felt more comfortable with Bacon's style of visionary science and his concern for the ends to which scientific method would be put than with Darwin's methodical sifting through factual evidence and slowly elaborating hypotheses. Like Bacon, Eiseley's strongest talents were as a "refiner" rather than a "miner" of scientific truth.

Though Eiseley's interest in Sir Francis Bacon naturally predated the event, an invitation from the University of Nebraska to give the Montgomery Series Lectures in 1961, while he was on leave from Pennsylvania, gave him the opportunity to cast his reflections in three lectures, later published by the University of Nebraska Press. Eiseley also used the second lecture in the series, "Francis Bacon as Educator," for an address at the University of Pennsylvania Faculty Club on January 23, 1961, at the commemoration of the four hundredth anniversary of Bacon's birth.[2] The first lecture, "The Man Who Saw Through Time," also appeared that spring in the *Saturday Evening Post* before the scheduled publication of *Francis Bacon and the Modern Dilemma,* as Eiseley originally entitled his book.[3]

As preparations for book publication of the lectures went forward during the spring of 1961, the working relationship between Eiseley and his editors at the University of Nebraska Press unfortunately broke down. Through a series of misunderstandings, Eiseley submitted his manuscript late and was in turn dissatisfied with the feeble proofreading and editing, which introduced a number of errors into the first edition.

Eiseley found over a dozen substantive errors in chapters 2 and 3, a discovery which led him to telephone Chancellor Clifford Hardin of the University of Nebraska and request that the entire edition be destroyed—since the quality was unacceptable to him—and that the venture be terminated. He even offered to return the entire sum for the Montgomery Lecture Series, provided that all future rights to the material copyrighted by the Press be returned to him. Chancellor Hardin responded with a proposal to reprint a new, corrected edition of the volume, to which Eiseley agreed, although before that work could be undertaken some of the 1,500 copies of the original edition were distributed to libraries and reviewers. When Eiseley learned of this he immediately sent a second letter of protest to the chancellor's office, and the agreement was apparently canceled, since the University of Nebraska Press never reprinted *Francis Bacon and the Modern Dilemma.*[4]

Ten years later, Kenneth Heuer, Eiseley's editor at Scribner's, obtained the rights to the book and it was reissued, along with an additional

chapter, as *The Man Who Saw Through Time*. This was the only edition that
Eiseley ever officially acknowledged, and the extant copies of *Francis
Bacon and the Modern Dilemma* have become collector's items. The entire
affair left Eiseley "heartsick" and determined to deal only with commercial
publishers in the future.

Because of its brevity, *The Man Who Saw Through Time* might best be
considered an introductory appreciation of Sir Francis Bacon, rather than a
full-length treatment of his life or works. In the first three chapters,
Eiseley briefly reviews Bacon's life and his position in Elizabethan society,
which he calls "an age of violence," and then discusses the "hidden world"
of the inductive method that Bacon bequeathed to modern science. The
third chapter, "The Orphic Theatre," deals with Bacon's contributions to
anthropology and other areas of scientific understanding, such as his
symbolic interpretation of the fable of Orpheus as representing the power
of human custom to subdue man's more primitive nature. Bacon also
warns against the dogmatic misuse of science in *The Advancement of
Learning,* in his analysis of the four kinds of misconceptions that divert
men from the truth. He placed the philosophical system of science under
his fourth category, the "Idols of the Theatre"; hence Eiseley's title, "The
Orphic Theatre."

Bacon's three essential insights, according to Eiseley, were his distinction between the lurking novelty in nature that man exploits and the
natural world undisturbed by human influence; his sense of man's un-
exhausted power not only to live in but to re-create nature, or bend the
natural world to his will, through the right use of reason; and his
"powerful sense of time," shared by Eiseley, which forced men to confront
the future rather than to continue worshipping the past. These, of course,
became major themes in Eiseley's works as well. In his preface, Eiseley also
distinguishes between Bacon's three uses of the term nature, all included
under the category of "natural history":

He counsels us, indeed, that we must distinguish between the normal *course* of
nature, the *wanderings* of nature, which today we might associate with the
emergence of the organically novel, and, finally, the "art" that man increasingly
exerts upon nature and that results, in turn, in the innovations of his cultural
world, another kind of hidden potential in the universe. (14)

Eiseley's purpose throughout the book is to defend Bacon's reputation
against those critics who, taking their cue from Macauley's Victorian

attack on his character, denigrate his lack of specific inventions or scientific discoveries. Bacon was neither an unscrupulous or corrupt counsellor nor a scientific impostor. Instead, he was a visionary, a prophet of science, and in Eiseley's concluding chapter, "Strangeness in the Proportion," he makes an articulate plea for the tradition of literary naturalists who have continued Bacon's work. The chapter title itself comes from Bacon's comment in his essay "Of Beauty": "There is no excellent Beauty that hath not some strangeness in the proportion."

"Science among us is an *invented* cultural institution," Eiseley reminds us, "as capable of decay and death as any other human activity, such as religion or a system of government." Moreover, it is a complex and demanding cultural activity, difficult to sustain. Bacon both invented the methods of modern science and anticipated its dangers. In *The Advancement of Learning* he wrote, "this is the foundation of all, for we are not to imagine or suppose, but to *discover,* what nature does or may be made to do." He was, in Eiseley's words, "the first great statesman of science," envisioning both the scope and methods of modern institutional scientific research, in which the labors of many minds devoted to a common problem, in a climate of steady accumulation and sharing of scientific knowledge, might overcome the dependence upon "the sporadic appearance of genius." "What Bacon lacked as an experimenter," Eiseley concludes, "he made up for in his range and vision of what science in its totality meant for man."

Above all, Bacon firmly believed throughout his life in the value of learning. As a young man he had remarked precociously in a letter to his uncle, Lord Burghley, that "I have taken all knowledge to be my province." True to his word, he later set about the monumental task of creating a model for reforming and reorganizing the antiquated system of medieval learning, in his treatise *The Advancement of Learning.* This new system would be based upon inductive analysis, practical understanding, and the utility of knowledge. His purpose was to overturn the narrow scholastic system then dominant at Oxford and Cambridge and replace it with a new system of secular learning based upon memory, imagination, and reason. "For the world is not to be narrowed till it will go into the understanding," he wrote, with respect to the Scholastic method, "but the understanding is to be expanded until it can take in the image of the world." With these words he threw open the windows to the stuffy world of the medieval university. The scientist, rather than the philosopher or theologian, was to be his model of the learned man, though his humane science would still combine compassion and understanding.

Bacon emphasized, moreover, that there are twofold truths—those of science and religion—which must not be confused, since one cannot be used to "prove" the validity of the other.[5] Yet as Eiseley argues in his concluding chapter, that distinction has not always been honored, either by the forces of knowledge or faith, with respect to each other's proper domain. In our time, especially, experimental science has tended to create its own metaphysic, one which restricts truth and reality to empirical limits. "Authoritarian science" has replaced "authoritarian religion." Bacon envisioned that his "engine" of science would remain the servant, not become the master of man. Yet "in his enthusiasm for a new magic," Eiseley observes, "modern man has gone far in assigning to science—his own intellectual invention—a role of omnipotence not inherent in the invention itself." In doing so, he has struck a Faustian bargain with the future. Central to Eiseley's thesis is the metaphor of the "crossroads" that our scientific culture has reached, where either we find a way to encourage the growth of human responsibility adequate to control the powers that science has placed in our hands, or man will surely perish. Science itself will not necessarily save us, because, through what D'Arcy Thompson called "the evolution of contingency," new technological inventions in turn create new problems. In a concluding gothic incident that he surely imagined, Eiseley recalls once encountering a stranger in a remote rural area, and he compares modern man to the desperate figure he saw atop a swaying haywagon during a violent storm, trying to control his runaway horses while searching for a signpost to point the direction for him. This mysterious figure, with a dual countenance—serene and demonic—represents modern man groping his way toward an uncertain future, a future compounded of hope and despair. Eiseley felt increasingly that the intuitions of our literary natural history writers were a surer guide to the future than the prognostications of science, so he turned his literary energies almost exclusively to the essay, poetry, and autobiography during the last ten years of his life.

The Unexpected Universe

In his next major book, *The Unexpected Universe,* Eiseley once again worked with his old friend and former editor, Hiram Haydn, who in the meantime had moved from Random House to Harcourt Brace Jovanovich. Yet their second collaboration somehow lacks the tight unity, smooth thematic transitions, and overall coherence of *The Immense Journey,* though it does contain essays of individual distinction and beauty. Though both books were essentially shaped from previously published essays—a common Eiseley practice—*The Unexpected Universe* does not reflect the same degree of success in revising the separate essays to provide the transitional links—both stylistic and thematic—evident in the earlier work. Eiseley probably should have included a preface or introduction to *The Unexpected Universe,* making his themes and preoccupations clear to the reader, or else, in later editions, he might have used an essay by poet W. H. Auden which instead introduces *The Star Thrower.* As it stands, his major themes can be intuited from the first chapter, but they are more elusive and subtle than those in *The Immense Journey.*

Eiseley probably began *The Unexpected Universe* during the 1963–64 academic year, after he was awarded a Guggenheim Fellowship, although his grant application suggests that he was also planning an intellectual autobiography during this time. Subsequent grants from the Institute for Research in the Humanities at the University of Wisconsin and the Menninger Foundation allowed him additional working time to complete the ten essays, many of which appeared in print before the book was published. Eiseley was of course adept at placing his essays with a variety of magazines as a way of extending his readership and getting more exposure for his work. It should not be surprising, then, if his basic unit of composition was the essay (or chapter) rather than the book-length nonfiction form. Often his essay collections seem like afterthoughts, since the books were usually assembled from recently published essays rather than being planned and written as a single unit. Few of his books were explicitly written as such, perhaps only *Darwin's Century* and *All the Strange Hours,* the rest being editorial assemblages, though some works, such as *The Immense Journey, The Invisible Pyramid,* and *The Night Country,* still achieve a notable unity of theme, tone, and style. Often the unity achieved was the result of careful and extensive revision and rearrangement of the essays, with some even being completely reorganized. Evaluation of Eiseley's prose, it would seem, should begin with these assumptions: that he was basically an essay writer, though perhaps one of the most eloquent stylists of this century to work in that genre, and that his books should be approached as anthologies or collections organized around a common theme rather than as extended nonfiction works.

The loose, episodic structure of *The Unexpected Universe* reflects the dominant allusion to Homer's *The Odyssey,* itself a loosely organized set of episodes that chronicle Odysseus's adventures during the ten years it takes him to wander back to Ithaca after the Trojan Wars. Even though the story of modern science may assume epic dimensions, it is neither a completed story, in the sense of a classical epic, nor a thematically unified one. Hence the open structure and the tentative mood of *The Unexpected Universe* are appropriate for such personal revelations as Eiseley wished to share with his readers.

The unity of the book derives from the voyage motif and the sustained allusion to the figure of Homer's Odysseus and the subsequent literary interpretations of the "Ulysses theme," particularly Giovanni Pascoli's melancholy "Ultimo Fiaggio" [The Last Voyage], published in 1904. The dominant persona in all of the essays, however, is Eiseley, speaking as the disillusioned scientist-Ulysses figure, who has embarked on a personal "quest" to resolve his doubts about the limitations of science. This unifying purpose is confirmed in the book's proposed subtitle, "The Odyssey of a Scientist," which was never used. The voyage motif links the various essays through Eiseley's use of a variety of imaginary landscapes—beaches, shorelines, and coasts—which he creates as the settings for the "numinous encounters" that illuminate his personal universe. Through a series of allusions to Odysseus, Captain Cook, Darwin, and finally Eiseley himself, the book's "voyage" progresses from legend, to history, to science, and finally to the inner life, as each explorer-voyager sets out upon a quest shaped by the forces that impel him: the hunger for adventure, the desire for fame, the drive of intellectual curiosity, or the search for inner tranquillity.

The figure of Odysseus dominates the book since Eiseley views him as the prototype of the modern man of science, recognizing, as Dante had previously, the dangers inherent in his eternal hunger for new discoveries and fresh experiences. The greatest danger arises of course in the Baconian linking of knowledge and power, so that the quest for knowledge becomes a disguised drive for power rather than a disinterested pursuit of knowledge for its own sake. It is perhaps no accident that two of the most potent and enduring Western myths—those of Ulysses and Faust—both warn against the serious consequences of unrestrained hunger for knowledge. Dante places Ulysses in the twenty-sixth canto of his *Inferno,* where he is embodied as a flame, suffering the eternal torment reserved for fraudulent counsellors. To the medieval world he possessed an inordinate desire for knowledge and experience beyond that permitted for man—an apt symbol for modern science. Faust also shares Ulysses' desire to know, without having his courage and hardihood, so this cloistered and disillusioned scholar is easily outwitted by his genial tempter, Mephistopheles, despite Gretchen's attempt to intercede for him with the Almighty. If Odysseus represents the heroic, then Faust personifies the demonic side of the Janus face that is modern science. Each is present, often in the same person, as Eiseley seems to imply in his inscrutable encounters with mysterious strangers who so often seem to be psychic projections of himself. Yet Eiseley also incorporates the qualities of a third Western legendary figure, St. Francis of Assisi, who embodies qualities of compassion and love for the rest of the natural world not found in Ulysses or Faust.

The story of eighteenth- and nineteenth-century science is also an epic journey, culminating in the rediscovery of the lost history of life, as Eiseley reminds us in chapter 2. In our age, the attractions of space discovery and the seductions of objectified knowledge compete with man's desire for inner comprehension and peace of mind. These outer and inner drives create man's eternal dissatisfaction with his state and his restless desire for the ever-new knowledge and discoveries that he erroneously believes will provide for him the satisfaction he craves. "The Ghost Continent," that hidden world within each of us, symbolizes the disguised nature of our desires and our profound lack of knowledge of ourselves. Instead of additional space explorations, Eiseley proposes an inner journey of meditation and contemplation to regain the magic of wonder in "an impoverished age." The essays that follow constitute a loosely associative record of the oracles and "natural miracles" that he discovers during that "voyage."

Above all, Eiseley's "unexpected universe" possesses two qualities : it is personal and unempirical. The book announces itself as a "personal voyage" or "journey" to these self-discoveries, establishing an extended metaphoric comparison between Odysseus's adventures, Cook's voyage to Antarctica, Darwin's discoveries, and Eiseley's personal quest to explore the "ghost continent" within himself. Geographic metaphors bode large in Eiseley's musings as a means of illustrating the boundaries between conventional knowledge and the rich insights that Eiseley offers; this is very much a book about "boundaries" in the sense of the distinction between empirical knowledge and humane wisdom. Each essay contains a record of his encounters with unexpected and symbolic aspects of the universe, ranging from seeds and the hieroglyphs on shells to a deer mouse in a lecture hall, a dying gull on a reef, Ice Age artifacts, lost tombs, an attendant at a city dump, a fox cub on a beach, even the blood cells that he lost after a fall. All of these incidents are bound together by the common theme of desolation and renewal in nature.

It might be useful to consider the ten essays in *The Unexpected Universe* as a series of prose meditations, or thoughts directed at the cultivation of a specific emotion or state of mind—one that might best be characterized as a mixture of awe, wonder, and compassion—through a successive appeal to memory, understanding, and will. Like Wordsworth, whom he so much resembles in his use of memory, Eiseley recalls key incidents to describe the growth of his compassionate wonder toward the natural world. As his use of an epigraph from Heraclitus suggests, Eiseley implies that if you do not expect the unexpected, you will never find it. His preparation for these gratuitous encounters consists in divesting himself of his scientific skepticism and learning to recognize the unexpected as it occurs.

Because these essays attempt to encompass so much, a blurring of genres takes place which makes them difficult to define. They range from autobiographical incident to history of science to physical and cultural anthropology to a variety of literary allusions. Often they seem to be little more than extended "free associations," as one reviewer has called them.[6] An Eiseley essay at its best depends upon a fine balance of autobiography, allusion, and exposition. The allusion often sets the theme, the exposition introduces the conceptual material, usually scientific, and the autobiographical incidents provide tone, structure, and continuity. The essay will not "work" if one or more of these elements is out of balance—if the exposition is too lengthy or repetitious, if the autobiographical segments seem contrived or sentimental, or if the allusions are too obscure. The finest essays in *The Unexpected Universe,* perhaps "The Star Thrower," "The Angry Winter," and "The Innocent Fox," all maintain this precise stylistic balance, with a key autobiographical episode providing the foundation for Eiseley's more abstract speculations. Each reveals a desire to reverse "time's arrow" and to recover the miraculous through the lost world of the child.

Eiseley may well have considered parts of *The Unexpected Universe* as a series of "rehearsals" in autobiography. As the final stage in the set of voyages he envisions from outward adventure to inward contemplation, autobiography becomes a personal epic, a record of how well Eiseley has "endured" his life. Hence, the autobiographical sections of these essays comprise the most memorable passages in the book. In these sections, Eiseley's technique is to confront us with a mystery, a "numinous encounter," without suggesting a pat resolution. Most scientists scrupulously exclude anything personal from their writing, but Eiseley makes science an intensely personal and often mystical experience, as he re-creates selected incidents from his career. All of these incidents brought him face to face with a "Mysterious Other"—miracles, one might almost say, that forced him to contemplate the subjective and illusive dimensions of the natural world. As a scientist he had been trained to consider them only in rational, objective terms, but Eiseley moves beyond the realm of science in these essays.

In his splendid appreciative essay, W. H. Auden observes that Eiseley was "a deeply compassionate man" who, in his own words, "loves its small ones, the things beaten in the strangling surf, the bird singing, which flies and falls and is not seen again." This fellow feeling, which Eiseley wryly calls "a renunciation of his scientific heritage," leads him to "love the lost ones, the failures of this world." Through this compassion, "he reveals himself," in Auden's words, "as a man unusually well trained in the habit of prayer, by which I mean the habit of listening."[7] Eiseley's gift for careful listening implies an openness to the Word, the Spirit, not usually found in scientific minds accustomed to observe and record with detachment. These "numinous" encounters often involve strange and solitary figures, shamans perhaps, bearing oracular messages decipherable to a mind open to such preternatural events.

Another curious quality about these episodes is that many of them have been heightened or altered to suit Eiseley's thematic purposes—and some may be largely invented to fit the context of a particular essay. Eiseley admitted in response to a query about the name Costabel: "I picked it up by listening to a seashell many years ago somewhere on what has sometimes been called the coast of illusion."[8] Clearly, these autobiographical passages, which seem so disingenuous and candid, are actually highly contrived literary efforts. The name "Costabel," for instance, which suggests an imaginary Caribbean island or tropical resort, resembles Cristobal, the name of a Pacific port city in Panama; but perhaps more importantly it has strong Coleridgean overtones. Like Coleridge, Eiseley preferred to use timeless, imaginary settings for his most personal utterances.

Another such imaginary projection of great emotional import to Eiseley was the creation of "Wolf," the shepherd dog, who is featured in "The Angry Winter," and to whom *The Unexpected Universe* is dedicated. Apparently, no literal dog by that name ever existed in Eiseley's life; instead, "Wolf" represents the embodiment of all of the dogs that Eiseley ever wished to own, but could not, because of his mother's dislike of animals, his poverty, his transient life, and his later dwelling in apartments that prohibited pets. Eiseley invested so much feeling in "Wolf" that his creation gradually assumed a life of its own, as a kind of fictional companion for him. So intense was his imagined kinship with this creature that *All the Strange Hours* ends with Eiseley visualizing his own death, in some uplands Ice Age landscape, with only "Wolf" for a companion when his end arrives. This relationship with "Wolf" also epitomizes early man's kinship with the newly domesticated creatures that shared his fire and whatever scraps of food were tossed their way. The intensity of that rapport is also reflected in "The Ghost Continent," in Eiseley's accounts of the reunion between Odysseus and his dog "Argos" and between Darwin and his favorite dog after his five-year absence; it is a projection of that original, primordial bond between man and beast that reaches out to modern man with the reminder not to forget his fellow creatures or "the green wood" from which he sprang.

From these "rehearsals" in autobiography came a reaffirmation of his kinship with the transcendentalist Thoreau rather than the pragmatist Darwin. Like Thoreau, who confronted the cultural barrenness of nineteenth-century America and responded to the lack of available cultural myths by evoking the mythic dimensions of his own experience, Eiseley also became increasingly a personal mythmaker, forging a mythic personality (of the scientist as seeker) from the cumulative autobiographical material woven throughout his writing. What is most apparent in *The Unexpected Universe* is Eiseley's shift in identity from a scientific to a literary role—from Darwin to Thoreau. During the 1960s he was clearly establishing himself as a literary naturalist, regardless of the cost to his scientific reputation. As he comments in a letter from an admirer comparing him to Antoine de Saint Exupery, "Being a scientist who frequently writes in that no-man's land between science and literature, I find myself sometimes misunderstood, castigated, or denounced as a 'mystic.' One simply has to remember that there are people who hear with other ears. . . ."[9] That note of Thoreauvian independence would become even more apparent in *The Night Country* and *All the Strange Hours,* the two versions of his spiritual autobiography, but first came an intervening book in response to the NASA Apollo space mission that Eiseley called his "moon book."

The Invisible Pyramid

Given Eiseley's humanistic outlook and his skepticism about technological "progress," he inevitably would have had deep reservations about the value of the American space program. As early as 1968, Kenneth Heuer, a science editor at Scribner's, had contacted Eiseley about the possibility of writing a book on the evolutionary and philosophical implications of the Apollo 11 moon landing that was soon to take place. Eiseley agreed and signed a multiple contract with Scribner's to cover *The Invisible Pyramid* and two additional original nonfiction works. He also proposed to edit and write introductions for at least three works in a projected history of science series that Scribner's was planning. The titles mentioned were Darwin's

The Formation of Vegetable Mould Through the Action of Worms, Helmholtz's *Ice and Glaciers,* and Huxley's *On a Piece of Chalk,* although apparently only the Huxley text was ever published (1967).

During his association with Scribner's Eiseley also began a productive collaboration with a series of artists who would execute the woodcuts and illustrations for all of his books that the firm published. Eiseley seemed to favor the work of Walter Ferro, who illustrated *The Invisible Pyramid* and *Another Kind of Autumn,* and Laszlo Kubinyi, whose sensitive line drawings grace *Notes of an Alchemist* and *The Innocent Assassins.* Eiseley also chose Leonard Fisher to illustrate *The Night Country* and Emanuel Haller to produce the artwork for *All the Strange Hours.* These Scribner's hardcover editions, along with the award-winning limited edition of *The Brown Wasps,* illustrated by Jack Beal and published by Walter Hamady's Perishable Press in Wisconsin, all testify to Eiseley's aesthetic concern for handsome typography and layout in his later works.

The Invisible Pyramid gradually took shape between 1968 and 1970, during which time several of the chapters were delivered as lectures (in the fall of 1969) under the auspices of the John Danz Fund at the University of Washington in Seattle. The first chapter, however, originated as "The Freedom of the Juggernaut," which Eiseley delivered at the Mayo Clinic in 1964. Eiseley later used an excerpt from chapter 6, "Man in the Dark Wood," for his Harvard Phi Beta Kappa Address on June 9, 1970, when he shared the podium with poet James Dickey, who recited his poem "Exchanges" at the ceremony. Most of these chapters also appeared in periodicals before the book was published, including "The Last Magician," which was printed in the August, 1970, issue of *Playboy.* Eiseley bemusedly noted in a letter to a friend that he earned as much from the one piece in *Playboy* as the entire royalty earnings from some of his previous books. Despite the earlier publication of individual chapters, *The Invisible Pyramid* still profits from Eiseley's careful attention to thematic unity and overall structure throughout its seven chapters.

Though ostensibly a commentary on the space program, *The Invisible Pyramid* estimates the value of our entire technical civilization and the environmental impasse to which it has brought us. It contains both the technical insight of Lewis Mumford's *Technics and Civilization* (1934) and the philosophical scope and temperamental pessimism of Freud's *Civilization and Its Discontents.* Unlike Norman Mailer in *Of a Fire on the Moon* or Archibald MacLeish in "Voyage to the Moon," Eiseley is not overawed by the technology of man's space achievements. Instead, he constantly raises questions about its unseen costs, both in natural resources and human

effort. While Mailer tries to capture the human or existential drama of the
Apollo moon flight, Eiseley searches for the hidden philosophical implications of this contemporary cultural achievement, which may perhaps be
our equivalent of the Egyptian pyramids. As a result, *The Invisible Pyramid*
sustains a pessimistic tone that contrasts markedly with most journalistic
commentary about the Apollo flight. One might even call it a book of
tragic insight in which Eiseley speaks of every great civilization's urge
toward transcendence and the inevitable limitations that bring about its
decline and fall. Eiseley balances the themes of physical transcendence
(space flight) against spiritual transcendence (inner spiritual growth) as
opposing, incompatible tendencies within our culture. The price of the
wrong choice this time, he implicitly warns, may be man's eventual
extinction.

Though differing profoundly in tone and outlook from Bacon's optimism about the uses of science, *The Invisible Pyramid* is perhaps Eiseley's
most "Baconian" book in the sense of using its sustained metaphors of the
"invisible pyramid" and the "cosmic prison" to describe man's cultural
edifice—his second nature—and its inevitable restrictions on his dreams
and aspirations. It is a book of paradoxical logic, exploring how man is
both restricted and liberated by those bonds of time, environment, space,
and mortality that constitute his "cosmic prison." The metaphor of cosmic
infinity and human insignificance is in turn broken down into a series of
smaller, more immediate "prisons" that limit man's ambitions. This
insistence on limits, at once so timely and yet so foreign to certain
American cultural attitudes, was perhaps inspired by Eiseley's response to
the hubris of a U.S. senator, who declared after the first moon walk that
"we are masters of the universe—we can go anywhere we choose." Man
does not, in fact, have any such freedom, Eiseley demonstrates. The worlds
of nature ("the sunflower forest") and man's technological culture ("the
invisible pyramid") are explicitly contrasted, with Eiseley urging a return
to, or at least a reconciliation with, the surrounding world of nature, since
as he argues, man has little practical possibility of ever leaving this planet
through space flight to find a more hospitable world, should he exhaust its
natural resources or irreparably ravage the earth.

Perhaps the most intriguing and disturbing image Eiseley conjures up
is that of man as a cosmic "spore bearer" and his great cities as planetary
"slime molds" that, having spread over the earth's surface and devoured
the natural environment, are ready to extend their towers and launch
"capsules" into space. Implicit in this comparison is the image of man as a
threat to the rest of nature—an organism that has seriously overextended

itself and therefore faces the possibility of extinction. Besides such figures as the poet Robinson Jeffers, Eiseley stands among the few contemporary writers who have seriously entertained the possibility of human extinction and viewed that prospect as a not entirely unmitigated catastrophe. After all, there is little to suggest that we are the last of nature's experiments.

Eiseley also feels that regardless of its propaganda value the space program has cost our nation untold human and financial resources that might better have been used to alleviate immediate social and environmental problems. One rocket launch, for instance, costs as much as endowing a new university. He is also puzzled by the romantic urge many feel to leave the planet earth, at least symbolically, through the promise of the space program, as if earth were threatening to destroy man instead of the reverse.

Returning to Bacon's vision of man's dual nature, Eiseley demonstrates that man has passed beyond the natural mode of existence in his evolution and now dwells within an artificial "world" of language, technology, and culture. Nevertheless, he has not escaped from the "green world" he has left behind. Rather than dreaming of intergalactic flight, man must find a way to reverse this cultural pattern of estrangement from nature—difficult though such evolutionary choices are to reverse—and return to nature with renewed compassion and understanding, following the teachings of the great axial religions. Eiseley envisions, as Bacon had also imagined, a benign harmony between science and nature. No longer can man simply migrate and leave behind the ravages of his culture; we are running out of space and there are no more unspoiled regions left to settle. Should our present technological civilization collapse, like the great sun empires of Central and South America, there would be no forests left into which man could retreat. Yet Eiseley retains some hope that man can learn to exist without having to exploit and destroy the natural world. For Eiseley as for Thoreau, the highest mark of civilization was not technical mastery but a culture's ability to live in harmony with its surroundings, not destroying what it enjoys. For both writers, nature is "more to be admired than it is to be used."

The Star Thrower

Eiseley's last literary project was to select the poems and essays for *The Star Thrower,* which was published posthumously. The book was edited and seen through the press by Kenneth Heuer, once the science editor at Scribner's, who had moved to Times Books. *The Star Thrower* is an anthology of twenty-three essays and ten poems, some previously unpublished, which span Eiseley's writing career. All the poems, with the exception of "Let the Red Fox Run," date from the 1930s and early 1940s, and none had been collected. The prose selections blend the familiar with the new. Nine essays are reprinted from *The Immense Journey, The Unexpected Universe,* and *The Firmament of Time,* while others range from fantasy and science fiction to magazine excerpts and lectures. Originally Eiseley planned a book in five sections, to be called *The Loren Eiseley Sampler,* but Heuer cut and rearranged the material into three sections.[10] The first thirteen essays appear under the heading "Nature and Autobiography," followed by ten poems; and there is a final group of ten essays under the title "Science and Humanism." The book takes its title from a chapter in *The Unexpected Universe,* appearing here as a separate essay. The volume is introduced by W. H. Auden's splendid appreciation, "Concerning the Unpredictable," reprinted from the *New Yorker* in slightly revised form.[11]

The selections in "Nature and Autobiography" offer some of the finest examples of Eiseley's prose as well as other miscellaneous pieces. Some are lesser items—pieces that did not fit into any previous books. They include material from the book rejected by Harper and Brothers that eventually became *The Immense Journey,* together with several early efforts at fantasy and science fiction. Though a few selections had never been published, most had appeared in magazines but were not included in Eiseley's books. Few of the unfamiliar pieces match his writing at its best, and they were all probably set aside for good reason. While the selections are individually interesting, the first section does not achieve the thematic unity usually found in Eiseley's books. At best, they introduce the reader to Eiseley and suggest his range of interests.

The ten poems in section two also seem rather out of place in *The Star Thrower.* All but one are early lyrics that should have been published in *All the Night Wings.* Here they seem misplaced and contribute little to what is basically a prose anthology.

The strength of this volume rests in the third section, "Science and Humanism," which includes a number of late essays on the institution of science and on relationships between the scientific and the literary imaginations. "Science and the Sense of the Holy" uses Rudolph Otto's concept of "the Holy" to explore the temperamental difference between two kinds of scientists and their approaches to science. The first view, typified by Freud, is that of the "extreme reductionist"—the complete skeptic and materialist—who refuses to acknowledge anything in nature beyond the empirically verifiable and who dismisses the sense of awe and wonder as childish fantasy. The other view, represented by Darwin and Einstein, acknowledges and respects these ultimate mysteries. In Eiseley's words:

Science as we know it has two basic types of practitioners. One is the educated man who still has a controlled sense of wonder before the universal mystery, whether it hides in a snail's eye or within the light that impinges on that delicate organ. The second kind of observer is the extreme reductionist who is so busy stripping things apart that the tremendous mystery has been reduced to a trifle, to intangibles not worth troubling one's head about. (190)

"A controlled sense of wonder" marks the beginning of a humane science, one that acknowledges its limits as well as its understanding. This attitude seems to be gaining more respect recently, as other scientists turn to the personal essay to share their views with a lay audience. It is what Lewis Thomas perhaps exemplifies in *The Medusa and the Snail*: the medusa is nature, the snail us. Despite our advances in science, we will never understand all of her manifold shapes and disguises. But wonder and compassion are also important in themselves, as humane attitudes, without which the best part of us is dead. Eiseley concludes the essay with a reinterpretation of *Moby-Dick* as an ecological parable about the struggle between these two attitudes: that of the "star thrower" or man of compassion and the "modern vandal."

"The Illusion of the Two Cultures" continues this attempt to define a humane science. Eiseley finds the "two cultures" issue to be more a matter of attitude than substance; it is an "illusion" created by the narrow professionalism of both humanists and scientists. Their common problem is the denial of the imagination by men who, in Santayana's words, "would wish to escape from the imagination altogether." This problem is magnified by two related assumptions: "that accretions of fact are cumulative and lead to progress, whereas the insights of art are, at best, singular, and lead nowhere, or, when introduced into the realm of science, produce obscurity and confusion." Eiseley strongly objects to the scientific "puritanism" that shackles the imagination.

On the contrary, he reminds us, "creation in science demands a high level of imaginative insight and intuitive perception." Both the scientist and the artist deal in symbols. For the scientist, however, achievement is quantitatively measurable, while the artist's vision is unique, though it can communicate its power to others. Yet images from science may also profoundly affect the human imagination, as cultural metaphors, and the scientist must be prepared to grapple with these extensions of meaning.

"Evolution" and "relativity," for instance, are certainly both theories and metaphors. The world of science must put aside its fear and intolerance of the imagination and recognize that both types of invention—scientific and artistic—spring from a common source. Other thinkers, notably Jacob Bronowski in *Science and Human Values* (1956), have urged the same broadening of scientific discourse to recognize the common human values that the "two cultures" ideally embrace: a search for unity in hidden likeness, a desire to order experience, a habit of truth, and a sense of human dignity. Their work represents one of the most interesting cultural developments to emerge from modern science—the exploration of the areas in which science reaffirms rather than undermines humanistic values. Their books and essays demonstrate that fact and value need not be inevitably opposed: that they find their common ground in human wonder and imagination. But the problem itself is not new. Emerson and Thoreau had confronted the same issue and found another resolution in their meditative nature writing. Eiseley found himself increasingly drawn to the work of these idealistic thinkers, and three essays in *The Star Thrower* reflect this growing interest.

These titles, "Thoreau's Vision of the Natural World," "Walden: Thoreau's Unfinished Business," and "Man Against the Universe," were probably intended for the "modest volume on Thoreau" that Eiseley never completed. His interest was not so much in literary scholarship as in appreciation written from the point of view of "a naturalist and archeologist looking at the materials from a slightly different angle of vision."[12] His admiration for Thoreau had been registered in the poem "The Snowstorm" (title from Emerson), which opens with the quotation, "It is the first and last snows—especially the last—that blind us the most." Many another allusion to Emerson and Thoreau appears in Eiseley's work. Though he never completed his Thoreau volume, these essays in *The Star Thrower* indicated Eiseley's sense of his affinities with the nineteenth-century American romantic naturalists. He gave "Thoreau's Vision of the Natural World" as his address before the Thoreau Society in the summer of 1973 and read "Walden: Thoreau's Unfinished Business" for a Santa Fe lecture on Thoreau's archeological interests. Afterward he corresponded with Thoreau's biographer, Walter G. Harding, about several allusions in *Walden* that puzzled him. Eiseley also frequently used "Man Against the Universe" in lecture appearances during the last few years of his life.

With Emerson and Thoreau, the issue is not so much their influence as a coincidence of their thought with Eiseley's. Quite correctly, Eiseley insists in his autobiography upon the originality of his thought, pointing out that he did not return to literary studies until late in his life. Nevertheless, the parallel between his metaphoric style and that of Thoreau is unmistakeable. Like Thoreau, Eiseley was at heart a poet whose finest poetry often appeared in prose. Both were meticulous observers of nature for whom facts became "incipient metaphor and potential law."[13] As often in Thoreau's writing, Eiseley's observations ripen into metaphor through implied analogies or figurative extensions from the original image. Eiseley could look at the rifts and fissures of a Badlands formation and see an analogy to the convoluted surface of the human brain, which contains its own "fossil memories of its past." Even the structure of his essays is metaphoric, tracing out a dominant image with analogy and allusion to explore its figurative implications. The play of metaphor in the imagination fascinated both men; they were addicted to multiple vision, one that saw the natural world clearly and distinctly, though never in a reductionistic manner, but also saw beyond it to human nature. Both Emerson and Thoreau of course were constantly aware of the doubleness of nature and of the correspondence between natural fact and spiritual fact—between mind and nature—and Eiseley shared this appreciation. For him nature was a repository of time, out of which the human mind—nature aware of itself—had emerged. One of Thoreau's metaphors that especially delighted him was the comparison of Indian arrowheads to "mindprints" or "fossil thoughts." In his metaphor Thoreau had alluded to the secret of the artifact as the "humanly touched thing" in precisely the same way that Eiseley valued it. Not one of the archeological experts at a seminar Eiseley once attended could render so rich or apt an expression of the significance of their work. Thus Eiseley came to value the intuitive vision of the literary artist as much as the empirical knowledge of the scientist; or rather, he realized that both are necessary for the scientist who would express the significance of his discovery in adequate terms.

"Man Against the Universe" examines the convergence of Darwin and Emerson through the influence of the romantic movement on nineteenth-century scientific thought. Each grappled with the philosophical implications of evolutionary doctrine, though Eiseley finds Emerson's optimism more appealing than Darwin's perfunctory bow to divinity and nature's "progress towards perfection" at the end of *The Origin of Species*. Emerson realized as well as Darwin the ambiguous effect of the newly discovered past on human nature, yet he also saw nature equally the source of perpetual novelty and renewal as the stage for the grim Victorian spectacle of endless struggle, competition, and waste. Because Emerson saw nature as fluid rather than a succession of fixed forms, he was able to retain a serene faith in the self-renewing potential of nature, so that each species, each individual, is perpetually new. In this respect he was a forerunner of modern "process" philosophy. "Nowhere is anything final," Eiseley comments, even in the human mind, where "our very thoughts transform us from minute to minute, hour to hour," so that we are never the same. In such a world, there is no such thing as a fixed human nature. Yet in another essay, "The Lethal Factor," Eiseley finds this same adaptability the chief threat to man's survival. Because man retains no fixed image of himself, he is liable to drift with the currents of intellectual fashion, a victim of the passion, intolerance, rigidity, or pessimism of a particular age. We need to learn how to see through time steadily, with a timeless compassion and disinterestedness, Eiseley concludes, in order to save ourselves from the vicissitudes of cultural change.

Two short essays in *The Star Thrower* present the dark side of Eiseley's view of human nature. In "The Winter of Man," he recounts an Eskimo parable about fearing three things: the cold, things not understood, and the "heedless ones" among us. Nor has modern man entirely abolished this fear. He retains a "wintry bleakness" in his heart as a creature of the glacial retreats, though what we now fear most of all is "the ghost of ourselves" in our advanced weapons and our misused technology. "Man himself is a consuming fire," Eiseley writes in "Man the Firemaker," he is *Homo duplex*: "He partakes of evil and of good, of god and of man. Both struggle in him perpetually. And he is himself a flame—a great, roaring, wasteful furnace devouring irreplaceable substances of the earth" (51–52).

Eiseley retained a mixed view of human nature until the end of his life, envisioning at once gloom and hope in man's future. During 1972 he wrote two guest columns for the *New York Times,* "The Winter of Man" (January 16) and "The Hope of Man" (November 6), reflecting this dualism. Eiseley saw good reason for both hope and fear in the record of human history. In "The Hope of Man," written on the eve of the 1972 presidential election, Eiseley observed that the future does not merely happen; it is actively drawn from our own substance. Hope as well as fear can be found there. Man's entire history has been a fabric of crisis and man has always risked his hope against an uncertain future. "We are again threatened with the insidious Elizabethan malady of weariness," he writes, a malady Francis Bacon also addressed when he wrote about science as "touching upon hope." Bacon's words speak to our age. Returning to this message, Eiseley concludes:

May Francis Bacon's voice still speak of hope, not for man only, but of the survival of the planetary life without which our own lives are as nothing. The risk is there but the indomitable human spirit will cry "assume the risk." By it alone has man survived. And only those who know what it is to risk can understand compassion.[14]

Eiseley ends *The Star Thrower* on this same note of hope and compassion, despite the gloom that sometimes darkened his vision. "We would win," he wrote, "if not in human guise then in another, for love was something that life in its infinite prodigality could afford." Still, darkness seems to predominate over hope in his most intimate works, *The Night Country* and *All the Strange Hours.*

Chapter Five
A Fugitive from Time

"Though I sit in a warm room beneath a lamp as I arrange these pieces," Eiseley wrote in the foreword to *The Night Country,* "my thoughts are all of night, of outer cold and inner darkness." The same mood predominates here and in *All the Strange Hours,* the last two prose works he completed before his death. Perhaps some premonition of illness or the awareness of advancing age lent urgency to the task of completing his autobiography, but more than anything else the death of his mother loosed a flood of childhood memories and refocused Eiseley's attention on his painful youth.

After her husband's death in 1928, Daisy Corey Eiseley "skipped town," as Eiseley bluntly put it, and worked for several years as a household domestic in a number of small Nebraska farm towns, occasionally painting simple landscapes or still lifes to support herself. Finally she returned to Lincoln to live with her sister Grace after Loren's uncle "Buck" Price died in 1935. After he completed graduate school Loren supported both women, who rashly sold their home and moved into a series of "shabby rooming houses." But he saw little of his mother after his father's death. The pain of whatever lay between them may have been too great to bridge, or perhaps they had little left to share after Clyde Eiseley died. Loren clearly felt more affection for his father, but his mother exercised a powerful influence over his imagination and emotions, despite their long estrangement. In one of his notebooks he commented, "My mother was a woman who invited murder."[1] Even his autobiography seems more notable for what it omits than for what it mentions about this strange and tortured relationship.

Much of his impetus toward autobiography stemmed from his mother's death and funeral, which in 1959 brought the Eiseleys back to Lincoln for the first time in many years. With the reluctance borne of painful memories, Loren flew to Nebraska to arrange for his mother's funeral. He would not view her remains until just before the casket was sealed for the trip to Wyuka Cemetery, and even while he stood at her graveside the pain and heartache of all that remained between them left Loren unable to grieve. "Nothing, mother, nothing," he murmured, in a scene remarkable for its suppressed anguish. It was not callousness but extreme sensitivity and an unwillingness to relive the pain of past memories that left him so bereft of feeling. "Our debts would be cancelled only by my own death," he writes in *All the Strange Hours,* "and perhaps not then." Yet the funeral experience was doubtless cathartic, freeing his imagination to explore childhood memories.

Eiseley's notebooks suggest that plans for an autobiography had long been on his mind, but university obligations and other book projects prevented him from giving it his full attention, even after he resigned from the provostship in 1961. He outlined his plans for an "intellectual autobiography" in his 1962 Guggenheim application, but *The Unexpected Universe* actually materialized from that sabbatical.

While he was at Stanford's Center for Advanced Study in the Behavioral Sciences in 1961–62, he drafted an autobiographical lecture for the John Dewey Society on the purpose of education, entitled "The Mind as Nature." Here Eiseley set forth for the first time a brief account of his childhood in Lincoln; its purpose was to support the essay's theme that education can nurture creativity by compensating for childhood deprivations.

In a sense, Eiseley had been composing his autobiography intermittently throughout all his personal essays. One reviewer said of *All the Strange Hours* that "Eiseley has written this same book, under various disguises and titles, more than a half dozen times before."[2] Eiseley later admitted as much in an interview when he observed that his personal essays constituted a "continuing autobiography."[3] For this reason, when he came to write *All the Strange Hours,* he omitted much factual material and chose an impressionistic rather than a straightforward chronological account of his life. He felt he had simply told enough about himself elsewhere. What *The Mind as Nature, The Night Country,* and *All the Strange Hours* present are the probings and musings of a singular mind, like Montaigne's, directly and honestly accounting for itself; that is not the conventional story of a life. Taken together, the three books present an extended "spiritual autobiography." "Ironically," Eiseley comments in one passage, "I who profess no religion find the whole of my life has been a religious pilgrimage."

As in St. Augustine's or Rousseau's *Confessions,* or Wordsworth's *The Prelude,* Eiseley is primarily concerned with the growth of his mind and sensibility, and with explaining how he came to be as he was. He focuses on key incidents, or "spots of time" that point beyond themselves to some general moral or psychological theme. Often the precise context, his exact age, or the specific situation is less important than the impression the incident left upon him. Such "fictionalized" anecdotes often introduce more abstract or speculative thoughts through which the original incident assumes emotional and thematic significance. His autobiography enacts itself through his memory of significant moments, so that his identity resides in what memory has rescued from time.

Moreover, Eiseley often rearranges his experiences to give them heightened meaning. Because he is concerned with thematic significance rather than verisimilitude, Eiseley will sometimes change inessential facts or alter settings to lend his reminiscence greater dramatic power. Poetic license turns the memories of one child's world into fictional anecdotes which demonstrate the significance of childhood in the creation of the artistic sensibility. As in his powerful account in *The Night Country* of children stoning a turtle to death, a memory that later filled Eiseley with shame and disgust, his reshaping of the event points it toward the metaphoric. This particular incident recalls the pear-stealing episode in St. Augustine's *Confessions,* another childhood initiation to sin and evil. Eiseley, however, selects his childhood memories to illustrate scientific as often as moral precepts. This technique becomes explicit in *The Mind as Nature.*

The Mind as Nature

While Eiseley was on leave of absence at Stanford, Professor Arthur G. Wirth invited him to address the 1962 annual meeting of the National Society of College Teachers of Education.[4] Eiseley promptly agreed, glad for the opportunity to speak to a distinguished group of educators and share with them his thoughts about the teacher's role in encouraging creativity. He chose as his theme the value of education to compensate for childhood deprivations, using his own unhappy childhood as a prime example. The lecture and subsequent book he dedicated to Letta May Clark, "In gratitude for counsel and encouragement in my youth." The laconic dedication suggests how much Eiseley owed Miss Clark, a high school English teacher who recognized and nurtured his talent when he was scarcely aware of it himself, enabling him to transcend his surroundings and realize some of the potential he came to believe lurked unnoticed in the human mind everywhere.

The Mind as Nature presents a closely reasoned parallel between biological and cultural evolution, suggesting that the human mind also has its "natural history." The unseen potential for human creativity is likened to the genetic potential for mutation in nature. Creative genius expresses itself according to the same laws of contingency that operate in the rest of the natural world. Like the gene, the human mind has a "latent, lurking fertility" that the teacher—often in some mysterious way—can evoke. Education is thus a process analogous to natural selection, a kind of "cultural selection" by which the teacher selects and nurtures those traits that society desires in its children, but the educator must strike a fine balance between tradition and innovation as well as between the needs of the child's outer and inner worlds to encourage this emergent novelty.

Eiseley thus views the teacher as the primary agent of cultural change. More than that, the teacher is also a "savior of souls." The child lives in the present moment, while the teacher places bets on intangible futures, hopes that may never come true. Every experience for the child is instrumental in shaping a yet undetermined future. The teacher, continues Eiseley, "must fight with circumstance for the developing mind—perhaps even for the very survival of the child." In this uncertain struggle, a chance event may unlock hidden potential for the child, as when Loren wandered into the old University Museum in Lincoln and observed "a kindly scientist engrossed in studying some huge bones." The library, museum, and classroom did much to compensate for the cultural and emotional impoverishment of Eiseley's home; they eased that "solitude of an ice age" he endured as a youth.

Yet to Loren isolation and solitude had their uses. Without time to himself, he might never have developed those imaginative resources—his interest in nature, fossils, and man's origins—that provided an escape from the confinements of his home by creating a time and a place of his own. Artistic gifts are often released by loneliness and intense self-awareness. The child, once turned away from the world, reshapes external reality to meet his needs—and the literary genius continues that quest throughout adult life. As Eiseley demonstrates, "some degree of withdrawal serves to nurture man's creative powers. The artist and the scientist bring out of the dark void, like the mysterious universe itself, the unique, the strange, the unexpected."

But ordinary humanity fears the artist, perhaps in instinctive dread of the strange or novel. The artist's vision, product of his alienation, ensures his estrangement from the mass of men he wishes to address. When he holds a mirror up to society, its members often do not like what they see there. So, "like the herd animals we are," comments Eiseley, "we sniff warily at the strange one among us." Thus the teacher faces conflicting obligations: to nurture the exceptional student who will create vital innovations, and to produce the good citizens who will guarantee social continuity. As Eiseley observes, "the teacher is expected both to be the guardian of stability and the exponent of societal change." The educator's primary responsibility, nevertheless, belongs to the future shaped in the minds of the young. Out of the range of talent before him, the teacher must be able to recognize the potential scholars, scientists, or artists hidden in the personalities of such late-maturing, uncertain students as Eiseley himself had been in high school and college. Like Darwin, Einstein, Thoreau, Hawthorne, and Melville, such students may show little promise early in life. Where human creativity will manifest itself is a perpetual mystery, as John Dewey said, since there is no precise science of the individual. Neither is genius a purely biological phenomenon increasingly likely in larger populations. It is a rare, elusive gift.

Finally, Eiseley returns to the role of the educator in either enhancing or thwarting the advance of cultural evolution latent in the students before him. Teachers must fulfill John Dewey's vision of transmitting "their wisdom to the unformed turbulent future," but they must go beyond that as well. As Eiseley concludes, "if the mind is indigenous and integral to nature itself in its unfolding, and operates in nature's ways and under nature's laws, we must seek to understand this creative aspect of nature in its implications for the human mind." Chief among these "natural laws of the mind" is the constant emergence of novelty "with which education has to cope and elaborate for its best and fullest realization."

The editors at Harper and Row thought so well of *The Mind as Nature* that they approached Eiseley about publishing an expanded paperback edition if he would consider adding some additional essays to make it more substantial. Eiseley apparently demurred; the paperback edition never appeared, and he regained the rights to *The Mind as Nature* after the Harper and Row edition went out of print in 1966. With this text and other essays from *Harper's* magazine and elsewhere now in his possession, Eiseley contemplated a new book-length collection of his most memorable essays, organized around a common theme. By this time he was under contract with Scribner's; and, as soon as he had completed *The Invisible Pyramid,* he turned his attention to the book that was to become *The Night Country.*

The Night Country

The Night Country is a work recollected by night and haunted by time. The narrative voice, most distinctive in "One Night's Dying," is that of a lifelong insomniac, a night watcher and wanderer, a gentle and compassionate man, disillusioned with science, who turns to the personal essay to share whatever "natural revelations" he has to offer. His persona is that of the "fugitive," or in his animistic mask, the "fox," clothed in "the protective coloring of men." Using this persona, Eiseley takes us on a journey of descent, into the "night country" of his mind, past the ruins of memory and recollection. Time was the dimension he wished, as a fugitive, to cross. He had a strong atavistic yearning to live in the remote past, on the high plains or altiplanos of the West, among the campfires of primitive men.

The vision of Eiseley's "night country" begins with the nocturnal world most people instinctively fear—the world of bats, owls, rats, beetles, and other creatures that haunt the night. It starts with the "night tide" swirling about our feet and transforming even our familiar domestic animals into strange and grotesque objects, gleaming eyes that glare at us from the dark. It is a gothic world of watchful shadows and silent shapes.

An early outline of the book shows it taking shape as a disguised autobiography, "using the gloomiest night terrors, then beginning of the gold wheel, part of the night piece, the hobo story, [and] the years of science."[5] Ultimately it became a collection of autobiographical essays, organized around images of the "night country," the figurative landscape of Eiseley's mind. He considered calling his new collection *The Divine Animal* or *The Uncompleted Man* before finally settling on the more evocative title of *The Night Country*.[6] The book includes fourteen essays progressing from the anecdotal to the philosophical and meditative. The essays range from early pieces published in *Harper's* in the late 1940s or early 1950s to some written in the 1960s. Many of the original titles have been changed and some pieces have been revised to fit new contexts. Four of the essays appear in other Eiseley books, and several had been used as lectures. "The Divine Animal," an early version of "Instruments of Darkness," was delivered as the Blashfield Address at a joint ceremony of the American Academy of Arts and Letters and the National Institute of Arts and Letters on May 22, 1963, when Eiseley was inducted into the body. The year after its publication, *The Night Country* won the

Athenaeum Society of Philadelphia Literary Award for the best nonfiction
of 1971.

Beyond the gothic, the "night country" extends to elemental fears—
those irrational fears of childhood, of madness, of the unconscious, of
sleep, and ultimately of death. Eiseley's dark vision expresses our collective
fears of an uncertain future—of uncontrolled technology, environmental
destruction, nuclear war, and the possible destruction of man and all life
on earth. These are the particular demons of our age. While he cannot
exorcise them, Eiseley affirms that they can be kept at bay through St.
Paul's admonition to love, which "'Beareth all things, believeth all
things, hopeth all things, endureth all things.'"

But the darkness of his vision also came from a temperamental pessimism, rooted in his unhappy childhood, and little amenable to religious
consolation. Ultimately it traces back to his ambivalence toward his
mother and his fear of inheriting the deafness or irrationality that afflicted
her. For this reason his temporary bout with deafness in 1948 terrified
him. He began writing obsessively, during those long months of silence,
out of a desperate urge to communicate and push back the darker fears he
associated with loss of hearing. One can only guess at the trauma suffered
by a child whose mother is a constant source of anxiety rather than
assurance because of her incomprehensible affliction. Her behavior pained
and bewildered him and left him as much a stranger at home as among the
neighborhood children who shunned him as odd. Even with his father's
reassurance and his grandmother Corey's kindness, he was left emotionally
scarred. His temperamental mixture of hope and pessimism accounts for
the strangely compelling quality of such an essay as "One Night's Dying,"
whose tone seems almost self-contradictory, with St. Paul's admonition to
love followed by one of the darkest passages in all of Eiseley's writing:

How, oh God, I entreated, did we become trapped within this substance out
of which we stare so hopelessly upon our own eventual dissolution? How for a
single moment could we dream or imagine that thought would save us, children
deliver us, from this body of death? Not in time, my mind rang with despair;
not in mortal time, not in this place, not anywhere in the world would blood be
staunched, or the dark wrong be forever righted, or the parting be rejoined. Not
in this time, not mortal time. The substance is too gross, our utopias bought
with too much pain. (175)

Yet even here the gloom is tempered by a mystical act of empathy and
compassion, by which the exhausted and depressed Eiseley reaches out to
the old man shuffling through a foreign airport and mentally shares the

burden of his mortality, so that "one night's dying becomes tomorrow's birth." Without this glimmer of hope, Eiseley's work would be unbearable; with it we can accept the broodings of his dark imagination. What is most interesting in this and other essays in *The Night Country* is the prose strategy of reenactment through memory, which surely brought catharsis from the anguish he bore.

"The volume has no other purpose than to claim a time and to make it my own forever," wrote Eiseley in an unused preface to *The Night Country*.[7] His vision is distinguished by its acute awareness of time and its sense of man as a creature in time—newly evolved and still changing. "From some deep well below consciousness," he wrote in the same unused preface, "I must always have distrusted time and therefore I came to study it." In his most memorable essays he shows an exquisite sense of the passage of time, of changes too slow, too gradual, for most of us to notice. This sense of the steady, imperceptible movement of time, especially in its geological and biological forms, accounts for the gloomy, almost gothic quality of many of his passages; it calls to mind the equally gothic tone of Sir Thomas Browne's "Hydriotaphia, Urne-Buriall." Yet the darkness of Eiseley's vision is not simply a pensive melancholia for human mortality, the threat of oblivion, and the certainty of death. It expresses man's limitations as a time-bound creature who paradoxically yearns for the irrecoverable past as for the uncertain future. He envisions the ravages of time on a scale greater than human, including the elemental cruelty of nature and the contingency of natural selection. The darkness of his vision reflects the dark chaos from which life emerges. It recalls the nocturnal, arboreal worlds of man's prosimian ancestors. Finally, it represents the moral darkness, the savagery and barbarism, from which man is not yet free.

"Memory is the mortal enemy of time that flows," observes Eiseley, because from memory the writer may extract "spots of time" and, by endowing them with "symbolic life," immortalize them. From the image of Mickey's pawprints set in concrete to the more abstract, idealized sense of time and place that draws men and animals back to their familiar haunts in "The Brown Wasps," each of the essays pursues this illusion of somehow preserving memories outside of time in "the night country of the mind." The appeal to eidetic memory is as strong here as in *The Immense Journey*, and Eiseley uses the same techniques of selecting and arranging recollections to emphasize their metaphoric meaning. Paradoxically, while Eiseley the archeologist well understood the futility of all such efforts, Eiseley the artist derived his motive from this desire to create a refuge from time. This contrast in point of view runs throughout *The Night Country* and creates the mood of somber pathos with which Eiseley reflects on episodes from his life as a fugitive from time.

The flight from time had commenced early in his mind, he confesses, encouraged by the silent loneliness of his house and by his desire to escape from the noisy harshness of the outer, daylight world to the dark tranquillity of the imagination. In fact, Eiseley insists in "The Gold Wheel" that he was born a "fugitive":

> The world will say that this is impossible, that fugitives are made by laws and acts of violence, that without these preliminaries no man can be called a fugitive, that without pursuit no man can be hunted. It may be so. Nevertheless I know that there are men born to hunt and some few born to flee, whether physically or mentally makes no difference. That is purely a legal quibble. The fact that I wear the protective coloring of sedate citizenship is a ruse of the fox—I learned it long ago. The facts of my inner life are quite otherwise. Early, very early, the consciousness of this difference emerges. This is how it began for me. (4)

Three childhood incidents narrated in "The Gold Wheel"—the stoning of the turtle, the discovery of the gold wheel, and the escape on the tea wagon—define the stark world of hunters and hunted that he soon came to know. Told from the point of view of the child, each incident has been heightened or altered to convey a "poetic truth." All the innate savagery and barbarism of the pack emerges in the rough street urchins who turn on Loren with stones and fists after they have pounded the turtle to death. The horror drives Eiseley further into himself—to his world of solitary imaginative play and the discovery of the "gold wheel," a talisman of escape from childhood misery. His fascination with golden wheels launches him on his next adventure, when he tries to run away on the back of a brightly painted tea wagon, a brief excursion into the timeless landscape of the ordinary world transformed by the child's imagination.[8] But here again Eiseley is thwarted by "barriers," in this case a sudden storm that forces him to take shelter in a hedge in front of the bishop's house while the tea wagon disappears.

A fourth incident later in life finds Eiseley an unwilling hunter chasing an antelope across the open plains in a battered car, hoping for a "barrier" that will stop the driver's pursuit and allow the animal to escape. Hunter and hunted, posse and outlaw: these familiar images from the Western frontier are part of the instinctive ritual of the hunt that man has not yet outgrown. Eiseley's identification with the fugitive or hunted becomes even more apparent in *All the Strange Hours,* where it is a dominant motif. "Men beat men," an old drifter warns him, "That's all." The "night country" becomes his refuge from this endless pursuit.

In "The Places Below," the flight of Eiseley's imagination takes him back to the childhood world of caves and sewers, a descent into another realm of the "night country," one perhaps symbolizing the unconscious or the prehistoric. Along with another childhood friend, "the Rat," Loren explores the underground chambers of Lincoln's storm sewers, re-creating in their atavistic play the world of cavemen. Their games come to an abrupt end one day when a sudden rush of water sends them scurrying up through a manhole cover into the hands of Loren's disapproving father. "I suppose it must have happened that way when the Neanderthals left their caves for the last time," Eiseley comments, "with the big ice moving down." The mossy "Green Door" of another unexplored tunnel tempts them to return to these adventures, but the sudden death of his friend leaves this door unopened. Years later, on an archeological dig, he redis-covers it in the underground entrance to a king's chamber and identifies his urge to venture into it with the whole infinite backward yearning of the "ladder of life" to the primal caves or waters of darkness. Eiseley resists the impulse to enter this "Hall of Shadows" and reluctantly returns to the daylight. For all "fugitives from time," the mind is just such a cave, he intimates, with dark chambers and hidden corridors of memory.

The best of Eiseley's essays show a circular or spiral structure that moves from opening thesis to a series of anecdotes that enlarge the reader's vision yet ultimately return him to the essay's original premise. "Big Eyes and Small Eyes" shows just such a structure. It begins with a quotation from Conrad Aiken, which sets the tone for the piece, followed by a comparative anatomy of human and tarsier skulls, information introduced surrepti-tiously to support a major thesis concerning the fear that man, a diurnal animal, has of night. Eiseley then develops an image of the "night tide" that flows in with the evening and swirls around our feet, bringing with it the creatures of the night, particularly rats. He then tells two fictionalized anecdotes about rats, one concerning a large sewer rat that dropped onto the feet of a sleeping friend in a hotel room and another about a "greasy, wet-backed rat" who threatened to disrupt the elegant lawn party of a famous American novelist, who was at that moment holding forth on how man "'will turn the whole earth into a garden for his own enjoyment.'" "Conlin's rat," as Eiseley calls it, carries an ironic revelation from the night to mock the blithe optimism of the host's comments. Such night visitors remind Eiseley that man shares his daylight world with creatures beyond the bounds of his vision. The third anecdote, about the "black beetle," is self-consciously "gothic" and humorous. It concerns a strange visitor who appeared one night while Eiseley was deep in a book entitled *Demoniacal Possession* about supernatural familiars, though the beetle could not be found the next day when his wife thoroughly cleaned their apartment. A hobo story from his early years follows, in which he relates the experience of approaching a Western city by night and the shock of discovering how the darkness alters the shape, form, and behavior of a herd of range cattle and some guard dogs. It is, in short, about the shock of recognizing the familiar in a new guise and of having one's ordinary world altered by the power of darkness. Now, acclimated by a lifetime of insomnia, Eiseley greets these night dwellers as a fellow "demon," one with eyes adjusted to the "night country."

The earliest pieces in *The Night Country* are sketches dating from the late 1940s. They relate a series of incidents from his Western bone-hunting days or from his childhood and establish a frame of reference for the later meditations. Other pieces are reminiscences that use personal incidents as a springboard to more abstract speculations. In his most "Baconian" pieces, Eiseley develops logical arguments through allusions rather than anecdotal material. Perhaps his most polished and mature essays are meditations that interweave anecdote and reflection to develop a religious or metaphysical theme; here the anecdotes become almost metaphoric. In the structure of *The Night Country,* Eiseley mixes these essay forms in a contrapuntal organization, though the progression is roughly chronological from childhood to maturity, and from the early sketches to the more sophisticated forms.

"Instruments of Darkness" is one of the most richly allusive pieces in this collection. The essay develops the Baconian notion of the two natures, the external world and that "second nature" which man draws out of nature and attempts to impose upon the world. It contrasts those who accept nature as it is with those who wish to transform it, linking science and technology with magic as expressions of man's impulse to dominate nature and master time by predicting the future.

The allusion to the witches' prophecy in *Macbeth* serves as the control-ling metaphor in Eiseley's essay. The "instruments of darkness" refer both to man's misguided impulse to subdue nature and to our misuse of technology to this end. Eiseley warns us to beware the false claims of scientific omniscience, mere phantoms conjured out of our imagination, like the visions of the weird sisters that tormented Macbeth. Though the prophets of science may also conjure up half-truths, the future remains beyond human will to change, although it will depend largely upon what man chooses to believe about himself. Eiseley reminds us that "man's whole history is one of transcendence and self-examination" rather than prediction and control. Within the "night country" of the imagination, man's darkest problem remains himself. "The terror that confronts our age," Eiseley concludes, "is our own conception of ourselves."

"The Chresmologue," or parchment dealer, is perhaps the most abstract essay in *The Night Country,* dealing with man's changing conception of time.[9] Though related to *The Firmament of Time,* it traces the emergence of linear, noncyclic time in the ancient world, not the evolution of modern geological and biological time. Eiseley discusses the modern obsession with the future and our indifference to the past as signs of our insecurity and ignorance of ourselves. Like the ragged derelict Eiseley encounters on the train to Philadelphia, we have purchased a ticket to anywhere. This is the difference between modern time and Christian time; the Christian at least has a sense of eschatological purpose, a vision of the future that modern, secular man lacks. Our society turns not to religion but to the scientist, the modern parchment dealer or soothsayer, who deals in dubious prophecies to comfort a confused and doubting culture. The vision of any age is incomplete, Eiseley warns us, because as creatures of evolution "we are in the center of the storm and have lost our sense of direction." The future is within us, to be perpetually drawn forth from ourselves.

"Every ruined civilization is, in a sense, the mark of men trying to be human, trying to transcend themselves," Eiseley remarks in "Paw Marks and Buried Towns." Archeology was for him not simply the study of broken artifacts but the record of men scratching their initials in time. It was the study of how each civilization struggles to emerge from darkness and create enduring light and beauty in its cities and works of art. This study of man's record in time should inspire pity and humility, he muses, "for there is nothing more brutally savage than the man who is not aware that he is a shadow." Each civilization, each generation, must struggle anew to wean its young from their savagery and humanize them through education. The band of slum children armed with pointed weapons, whom Eiseley encounters in the outdoor courtyard of a university adjoining the slum, reveals the inability of our culture to achieve real civility in its cities. "Man will survive," he reflects wearily, "but in what shape or form he cannot tell. The darkness here represents the perpetual threat of man's reversion to barbarism without the enlightening influence of humane education. Eiseley returned to this theme repeatedly in lectures and essays during the 1960s and 1970s in response to university disruptions by those who would eschew the discipline of learning, or those who supposed they had nothing to learn from the past.[10]

"Barbed Wire and Brown Skulls" and "The Relic Men" are early sketches taken from Eiseley's bone-hunting adventures with the South Party. Each captures the rhythms and cadences of Western tall tales and humor. In the first piece, Eiseley explains his affection for skulls through three fictionalized anecdotes: the story of Uncle Tobias's skull, Loren's childhood museum of clay skulls, and the story of Old Mr. Harney and the skull of his Aunt Lucinda. The story of "Uncle Tobias," the distinguished lawyer with a penchant for skulls, foreshadowed the actual account of how Eiseley later came to possess the skeleton of Professor Edward Drinker Cope, a leading vertebrate paleontologist at the University of Pennsylvania in the nineteenth century, who left his remains to scientific research. After being misplaced for sixty years, the skeleton turned up in 1966 at the Department of Anthropology.[11] Professor Cope soon found a new home in Eiseley's office, where his bones rested in a "simple cardboard carton." Eiseley hoped that after his death Professor Cope's remains would be interred with his own.

The other early sketch, "The Relic Men," recounts the story of "Buzby's petrified woman," in which, reminiscent of Pygmalion, a lonely Badlands farmer falls in love with an oddly shaped stone concretion sculpted by the wind. The second anecdote tells of how the bone-hunters discover in a windy valley a major fossil quarry that Old Mullens, a devout Fundamentalist, takes for the remains of Noah's Flood.

Two of the longest essays in *The Night Country,* "Strangeness in the Proportion" and "The Mind as Nature," had appeared in Eiseley's other books or under separate titles of their own. Together they advance three themes: the danger of our faith in unexamined science and technology; the contemplative natural history essay as another way to comprehend nature; and the mystery of creativity manifest in even the darkest circumstances. Both the teacher and the natural history writer respond to the emergent novelty of nature as a promise rather than a threat. To that extent, each is free from our culture's fear of the future.

The two incidents in "The Creature from the Marsh" reveal the unseen forces of time at work in the present moment: historical time and evolutionary time. As Eiseley and his wife walk down a city street one day, he is suddenly visited by a fey sense of the city already crumbling and decaying in the present moment, of the living ruins. He imagines himself in the future, poring through the rubble of rusted metal and broken glass. "The terrible *déjà vu* of the archeologist" even permits him to visualize the bones of his wife's hand, pointing to an article in a shop window. "My sense of time is so heightened," he confesses, "that I can feel the frost at work on the stones, the first creeping of grass in a deserted street." Yet, because his science is an inexact one, he cannot answer impatient questions about the age and history of an ancient woman's skull brought to him for examination. His sense of time is acute but intuitive.

As a physical anthropologist, his specialty is "the time when man was changing into man," and he speculates about "missing links" in man's evolutionary ladder. In a tropical mangrove swamp, he unexpectedly discovers the "missing human link" in a mysterious set of footprints. Excited by his find, he crouches down to inspect them more closely—and discovers them to be his own! What terrifies him is the realization that no form of life, including man, is "final." All living forms blend and flow in evolutionary time, and "the creature from the marsh" is none other than himself.

The vision of Eiseley's "night country" culminates in his final pair of meditative essays, "One Night's Dying" and "The Brown Wasps." Here the central insight builds from a series of "natural revelations" Eiseley shares with the reader: "numinous encounters" that the insomniac night watcher returns to report. In "One Night's Dying" three incidents, one involving a broken-winged gull, the next a duck with a shattered wing, and the last a sick pigeon, provide momentary glimpses of the elemental cruelty of nature and of how wild things die. So also do old men shuffle off to meet death from the waiting rooms of the great urban railroad stations. Only compassion, Eiseley concludes, can save us from time's indifference to the pain of mortality. The sustained eloquence and intense feeling he evokes here place the essay among the finest examples of his prose style.

In "The Brown Wasps," Eiseley uses the prose strategy of reenactment through memory to assert each generation's right to its most precious memories, which alone save us from the ravages of time. "It is as though all living creatures, particularly the more intelligent," he comments, "can survive only by fixing or transforming a bit of time into space or by securing a bit of space with its objects immortalized and made permanent in time." Once again recollected incidents become thematic metaphors. The numbed wasps creeping slowly over their abandoned nest, the field mouse burrowing in an indoor flower pot, and the pigeons that flock back to a dismantled elevated railway station all prefigure Eiseley's attempt to recapture a moment from his childhood when he and his father planted a cottonwood sapling in their Nebraska yard. Sixty years later, when he returns to the town of Aurora, the tree no longer stands, though it has long stood in his imagination. Man and beast each "retained a memory for an insubstantial structure now compounded of air and time." Eiseley's homing instinct, as strong as that of the other creatures he describes, brought him back to Nebraska several times during the early 1970s, when he was engaged in research for his autobiography, *All the Strange Hours.*

All the Strange Hours

"Each man goes home before he dies," Eiseley wrote in *All the Strange Hours,* to push "through the cobwebs of unopened doors." While he was composing his autobiography, he returned to landscapes etched in his memory. Accompanied by his old friend Bert Schultz, now director of the Nebraska Academy of Science and himself a prominent paleontologist, Eiseley reexplored many of the collecting sites of the South Party, including the cabin mentioned in "The Bird and the Machine." He revisited his childhood homes in Lincoln and spent hours poring through old newspaper files to refresh his memory about the 1912 Lincoln prison break that figures so prominently in his autobiography. Being chosen for the Distinguished Nebraskan Award in 1974 may have made his return a sentimental as well as a literary journey for Eiseley.[12]

During this time, he was again on leave of absence from the University of Pennsylvania, although President Martin Meyerson assured Loren that he could continue teaching beyond the usual retirement age. This offer was a great relief to Eiseley, who for personal and financial reasons did not wish to retire. After he completed his award-winning autobiography in 1975, lectures and speaking engagements kept him busy through the fall of 1976, when he was first hospitalized with prostate trouble. He did not learn of his cancer until about six months later, when he developed jaundice during his recuperation. Doctors then discovered an inoperable cancer of the pancreas. Loren faced his final illness with great fortitude. Though he elected to risk a long and complicated operation, the cancer had metastasized. To the last he wrote letters and answered mail from his bedside. He died on July 9, 1977, at the University of Pennsylvania Hospital and was buried in West Laurel Cemetery in Bala Cynwyd. Memorial services followed at the University of Pennsylvania and the University of Nebraska in Lincoln. A particular poignancy about his death was that he did not live to see the return of Halley's Comet, as he had promised his father in 1910. During the last year of his life, he won two prominent awards: the Bradford Washburn Award from the Museum of Science in Boston for his outstanding contribution toward public understanding of science, and the Joseph Wood Krutch Medal from the Humane Society of the United States as "humanitarian of the year."

At the time of his death he had plans for a half a dozen new books, including a science-fiction novel, *Sea-Wolf,* to be set in the Ice Age.[13] The setting for this projected novel was a particularly appropriate one, since *All the Strange Hours* ends with the image of the fugitive Eiseley joining his dog Wolf and an Indian companion, "muffled in snow upon the altiplano." After his death, the most moving tribute came from his fellow writer Ray Bradbury, who said that Eiseley had simply "stepped down to lace his boots with ancient dogs and prairie shadows."

Eiseley's sense of himself as a fugitive from time is most pronounced in *All the Strange Hours.* Here the fugitive persona in all its dramatized forms—as escaped convict, hobo, drifter, gambler, trickster, scholar, and lonely child—controls the narration. The tone is established by a dominant childhood memory introduced early in the book and to which he returns at the end: a 1912 escape by three men from the Nebraska State Penitentiary in Lincoln. The convicts—Shorty Grey, Tom Murry, and Charles Taylor—fled during a March blizzard after murdering a brutal warden and blasting open the gates with nitroglycerin. They held out for less than a week in the bitter cold before they were finally surrounded by a posse near Fremont, where Eiseley's parents had lived when he was three. Eiseley first introduces this memory in response to a question W. H. Auden asks over dinner: "'What public event do you first remember from childhood?'" By the end of the book he imaginatively joins the escapees, identifying himself with Tom Murry, and disappears with them into the March blizzard. The book ends with him crouched with the other men, holding out against the posse, then falling and dying in the snow, only to emerge in the time he loved best, "on the cold bleak uplands of the ice-age world," accompanied by Wolf and the Indian. In life and in death he remained a fugitive, as he implies poetically in "The Double," leading the dual life of scholar and outlaw.

Eiseley's autobiography was more than ten years in the making. Part of his 1962 Guggenheim application stated that he was at work on an "intellectual autobiography" that would explore "certain aspects of a childhood . . . singularly deprived of intimate human contact."[14] A letter to Edwin G. Boring four years later (May 2, 1966) confirms that he was working on a "longer intellectual autobiography" as a sequel to *The Mind as Nature.*[15]

The original title for his autobiography was to have been *The Other Player: A Chronicle of Solitude,* but Eiseley later came across a line from

Swinburne's "Ave: Atque Vale" that he preferred: "Now all [the] strange hours and strange loves are over." Swinburne's poem, subtitled "In Memory of Charles Baudelaire," was occasioned by his visit to the grave of the French symbolist poet, whom he regarded as a brother, although they had never met. The Latin title, which means "Hail and Farewell," alludes to the elegy Catullus wrote after his farewell visit to his brother's grave. Likewise, the impetus for Eiseley's autobiography began, in a sense, with his farewell to his mother at her grave in Lincoln, an incident to which the book returns several times. Moreover, the first chapter opens with Eiseley's discovery of his aunt's vanity mirror after her death and seems preoccupied with what one reviewer called "death and darkness," offering an obituary for himself and his lineage.[16] A second volume of autobiography, tentatively called "The Immense Quiet," was planned but remained unfinished at Eiseley's death. It was to have ended with his wife and a friend "searching for him in living forms."[17] After its publication, *All the Strange Hours* received the Christopher Award for 1975 and was selected by the Book Council of the American Library Association as one of the notable books for 1975.

The epigraph comes from book 6 of Browning's *The Ring and the Book,* in which a crime and its perpetrator are examined from a number of perspectives, and it implies something about the nature of Eiseley's autobiography. Like Browning's poem, *All the Strange Hours* also deals with the unraveling of evil, spiritual and physical. An early notebook entry reads, "Autobiography organized around 'types of evil,' first verbal, second the hatchery—physical—corruption [and] malformation, my own sickness."[18] Another idea that appealed to Eiseley was arranging the chapters around the metaphor of "rings of memory"—immediate, intermediate, and long-term—analogous to the way the mind stores memories. But in the end he chose another metaphor, the mind as an "archeological ruin," a "rat's midden" of memories, stored in jumbled neural circuits.

"I require of each man a simple and sincere account of himself," wrote Thoreau; but Eiseley was too complex a personality to follow the prescription. Instead, *All the Strange Hours* narrates the growth of his inner life and glosses over external details. Eiseley shows a curious impulse both to reveal and to conceal, to tell the story of his life in such a fragmented, impressionistic manner that, while fascinating, it remains incomplete. Yet he insists that his story is important and worth listening to, and compels us to listen as he retells it repeatedly, from different angles, in his books and essays.

So unconventional a book as *All the Strange Hours* raises fundamental questions about the nature of autobiography. What, finally, is the purpose of the genre: to present the self in time, to justify one's existence, to account for one's life, or to retrieve the self from annihilation or oblivion? In Eiseley's case it seems to be to rid himself of an obsession—his dread of time—and to explain the sense of loss and dislocation that he had felt since childhood. Thus his life unfolds in a sequence more dreamlike than real. As a child he diced with Time for alternate futures. Later the trickster Fate returned in his various guises—dancing rat, Old Father Coyote, the Other Player—to cast the final throw. Since childhood he would gladly have fled from time had he but known where to run. There was nowhere to escape. "Running Man" he styles himself, always running—from his mother, the universe, himself. His whole life seems to have been a futile effort to comprehend time, from the toy crosses he planted as a child to his choice of a profession—anthropology and archeology—the study of man and his culture in time. The story of his life unfolds as Days of a Drifter, Thinker, and Doubter, through twenty-five chapters of terse narration.[19]

The controlling metaphor in this "excavation of a life" is archeological, justifying the fragmentary nature of Eiseley's narrative. He does not reconstruct his life as a continuous story but in a series of "memories, dreams, and reflections," arranged in an order of association rather than strict chronological sequence. Fragments of memory are all that have survived from the wreckage of his past. His mind resembles an archeological ruin, or tomb; and, in practicing "the terrible archeology of the brain," Eiseley attempts to reconstruct his fragments before they are scattered and lost: hence the image of the "shattered mirror" with which the book opens. The fragmentary narrative is not a deliberate evasion but a way of depicting the tricks of memory. Generally in autobiography "narrative continuity asserts continuity of self," but Eiseley does not claim that the continuously existing personality in time is an illusion, only that it is not accessible to memory.[20] His autobiography is an honest attempt to transfer what remains to paper before it is lost forever. The autobiographer is a "time trader," exchanging memories back and forth across the synapses of the brain. "Autobiographers are all liars," he once remarked, because the image of the self they present is only approximate.[21] Not the life but the memories that were most important in shaping that life are what the autobiographer reproduces. Autobiography is thus a selective art, Eiseley explains in a critical passage in *All the Strange Hours,* because it uses memories extracted from their context and endowed with "symbolic life" in the "unseen artist's loft" of the brain.

Writing an autobiography becomes for Eiseley an act of salvaging the ruins of self from effacement by time. His artistic motive is the same yearning for some form of transcendence or escape from time that gives the book its particular sadness and poignancy. Time becomes psychologically oppressive for him as an evolutionist who finds no escape from the prison of self, who thinks extinction the probable fate of man as a species, yet who feels his deep fellowship with all forms of life. This desire to escape from time shapes his narrative from the first chapter, which ranges through various levels of memory, beginning with a recent experience when Eiseley delivered the keynote address to the American Association of Museums.[22] His speech, "The Museum as Time Machine," and the blinding flashbulbs of the photographers, trigger a set of personal associations that launch his autobiographical narrative. The speech, which is not identified, is also metaphoric. The mind, too, is a kind of "museum" filled with relics and artifacts of memory. The same impulse to preserve motivates both the archeologist and the autobiographer: their common enemy is time. "Behind nothing, / before nothing, / worship it the zero," he says of time, quoting one of his own poems, "The Maya." For Eiseley "the most perfect day in the world" was the memory of an idle day during his years as a drifter when time temporarily ceased to exist for him and his companions. Later, during his first day in graduate school, the unendurable noise and confusion drove him into a Philadelphia cemetery, "with the sure instinct that time would vanish here."

All autobiographies involve a certain amount of self-dramatization in the act of shaping a life and imposing a pattern on past experience. As the writer emerges from childhood, recovers from some physical or spiritual crisis, discovers a purpose, records some accomplishment, and shares the vision of a purposeful, unified life, that particular life gains a retrospective coherence. To a degree, Eiseley shares this common autobiographical format, in his account of his recovery from tuberculosis, his struggle to finish college, his shaping of a distinguished career as a physical anthropologist and historian of science, and his discovery of his talent as a writer. Despite the element of chance, *All the Strange Hours* asserts the power of personality over circumstance. His life has not been so futile as the tone and mood of the book might imply, because his "excavations" have led him to a sense of deep humility and awe before the mysteries of life: the ultimate metaphysical questions that science cannot answer. His scientific training has given him a keen eye for fact and detail, though these yield image and metaphor in his imagination rather than hypothesis and theory. Eiseley could not abide the scientific separation of fact and value, and so he ultimately disbelieved in the orthodoxies of his profession. Therefore through his writing he presents us with a richer statement of what it means to be a human creature existing in evolutionary time.

As with the autobiographies of W. H. Hudson and Richard Jefferies, and with the journals and *Walden* that were Thoreau's continuing autobiography, Eiseley shares a naturalist's vision rather than a scientist's sense of achievement. If an autobiography is ultimately the record of how a writer takes the world and shapes it, then Eiseley's perspective came closer to that of a romantic naturalist than to the complacent materialism of Darwin's *Autobiography*. Eiseley shared more of Thoreau's gift for finding metaphors in "natural facts" than Darwin's genius for sifting through endless details and slowly assembling the massive evidence regarding the natural history of life. What makes Eiseley's literary vision distinctive, finally, is his pessimism about man and his tendency to identify with the nonhuman elements of nature, with his fellow creatures and with the elemental forces of nature.

Chapter Six
The Return to Poetry

Eiseley began and ended his writing career as a poet. Not only were his first and last published works poems, he was temperamentally more poet than scientist. Though his interest in poetry helps to account for his success as a prose stylist and as an innovator in reviving the familiar essay and virtually inventing a new popular idiom for scientific literature, his major accomplishment did not come in poetry. While his vivid imagery and lyrical voice distinguish his essays, his poetry did not benefit much from his scientific perspective. Once he had mastered his unique prose idiom, he employed it for poetry with little change; often his free verse and prose differ in little more than the arrangement of lines. Too many of his poems say with less ease and originality what he said better in prose.

His poetry suffered from a long period of neglect in mid-career, when Eiseley devoted himself to scientific and scholarly writing. Though perhaps he jotted occasional poems in notebooks, he published no poetry for more than twenty years. Therefore the poems fall into two distinct periods—early and late. The poems of his early career are traditional lyrics, sonnets, and narrative forms, which he wrote between 1927 and 1945. Those of his late period are mostly free verse meditations written after 1964, the greater number probably during the last decade of his life.

While in college he published poems in a number of small midwestern literary magazines, primarily the *Prairie Schooner,* which he joined as an editor in 1927. For more than a decade afterward he continued writing poetry and served as a contributing editor and poetry reviewer for *Prairie Schooner* and *Voices.* [1] As E. Fred Carlisle observes, "all serious young men, in a way, write poetry in college, but not with the care and skill of Eiseley." [2] After graduate school, anthropology demanded his attention, and he gradually abandoned poetry for scientific articles and the familiar essay. Not until the age of sixty-five did Eiseley publish his first volume of poetry, *Notes of an Alchemist* (1972), followed a year later by *The Innocent*

Assassins. Two posthumous volumes also appeared, *Another Kind of Autumn* (1977), prepared by Eiseley, and *All the Night Wings* (1979), a collection of early poems edited by Kenneth Heuer. Except for the ten poems in *The Star Thrower,* most of his early verse appears in *All the Night Wings.* The other three volumes—*Notes of an Alchemist, The Innocent Assassins,* and *Another Kind of Autumn*—and the last fourteen titles in *All the Night Wings* contain poems he wrote during the last decade of his life. At least twenty early poems and a few late poems remain uncollected.[3]

During his last decade Eiseley again began to send poems to magazines and journals. Occasionally he gave poetry readings at such places as the YW-YMHA Poetry Center in New York, the University of Pennsylvania, and the C. G. Jung Foundation. In 1975 the College of William and Mary invited him to read as the Phi Beta Kappa Poet at their annual Alpha induction. Though the publication of his poetry volumes was undoubtedly prompted by the success of his prose, Eiseley gained a measure of recognition for his poetic talent. W. H. Auden and Howard Nemerov admired his work enough to dedicate poems to him, and Eiseley returned the favor with a poem in *The Innocent Assassins,* "And as for Man," dedicated to Auden.[4] When Eiseley informed him about plans for a poetry volume, Auden responded, "'I shall greatly look forward to reading your poems. I know that, whatever else they may be, they are not going to sound like anyone else.'"[5] Nemerov remarked that Eiseley's essays and poetry seem to mirror each other, and called him "one of our necessary voices." But aside from appreciative reviews, Eiseley's poetry has received even less critical attention than his prose.[6]

Despite the recognition of his distinctive vision and his innovation in opening a new range of subject matter for contemporary poetry, the strength of Eiseley's poetic achievement remains uncertain. Vision and voice are separate critical questions: recognizing that a writer has something new to say is not to say that he has done it well. Eiseley's reputation is firmly established as a prose stylist, which is how most readers first discover him. Then perhaps they read his poetry. Even other poets seem to respond primarily to the "poetic" qualities of his prose. Too much of Eiseley's verse is a "poetry of ideas" in which the scientific concept is too weighty for the lyric or free verse form. As a result, the poetry expounds more than it sings. The poems read rather like broken lines of prose than free verse. Eiseley's poetry shows some of the same weaknesses as that of Thoreau, a "poetic" prose stylist whose pithy, aphoristic style seldom translated well to poetry. Indeed, Emerson's definition of poetry as "meter-making argument" suggests the risks of too easy paraphrase.

Though Eiseley's poetry has distinctive qualities, they are primarily those of vision rather than style. In his best poems he combines an anthropologist's perspective with his own acute sensitivity to time. Whether writing about nature or man, he introduces evolutionary perspectives that extend the poems backward and forward in time. He presents biological evolution as the "great epic of life," even though he did not write that epic himself. As a poetic interpreter of our prehistoric past, he has no peer in his ability to depict vast reaches of time. In the archeological poems, past civilizations seem as transient as "toadstools in the night." To the animal poems, perhaps his best, Eiseley brings a profound understanding of American Indian cultures, particularly of the shamanistic vision that merges man and animal in empathy. The animal poems move away from anthropocentrism to convey the experience of other forms of life on their own terms. Here the poems speak with real originality, introducing into poetic discourse nonhuman realms, treated with both sympathy and knowledge.

Eiseley's poems seem weakest when they attempt to duplicate what he does best in prose: when they lapse into poetic anecdote or self-absorbed reflection. The autobiographical poems are often discursive, lacking the rhythm and tautness of memorable poetry. He indulges emotions, risking pathos in excessive nostalgia. Eiseley was fortunate in that science taught him detachment and gave him a poetic matter beyond himself. Otherwise he might have been prone to the same excesses of self-indulgence which mar the work of other modern American "confessional poets," notably Lowell and Berryman: Eiseley lacked their ironic humor and ability to treat their own weaknesses with critical detachment. At their worst, Eiseley's poems are ponderous and didactic—essentially weaknesses of voice. Unlike Thomas Hardy's ironic detachment, which befitted both the novels and poetry, Eiseley's grave, meditative voice graces his essays but turns prosaic in verse. Techniques that worked well in the familiar essay did not carry over well into poetry. In *Notes of an Alchemist* and *The Innocent Assassins,* easy, graceful control of the poetic medium eluded Eiseley, whose prose style is by contrast superb in evocative grace and beauty. Not until his third volume, *Another Kind of Autumn,* did Eiseley achieve mastery of a poetic voice. In these late poems, many archeological in theme, he speaks in a quieter tone, with the measured rhythms of age, free from discursiveness. Voice and vision unify in elegies reflecting upon the transience of past civilizations—Egyptian, Minoan, Sumerian, Mayan—whose most enduring work could not outlast the ravages of time. He speaks with muted, impersonal eloquence of the impermanence of all things, natural and human, in a world of flux and change. These late poems perhaps represent his finest poetic achievement. As he remarked in "The Judas Tree,"

> I am like this tree.
> I come the closest
> to blossoming and sunlight
> now toward the end of winter
> when all I cherished is lost
> and I have no heart
> for summer leaves.

With the publication of *All the Night Wings,* both his earliest and latest poems are for the first time available in a single volume. Their thematic continuity, together with their change in voice and vision, mark Eiseley's growth as a poet.

The Making of a Poet

Later in life Eiseley claimed that he began writing free verse in high school, largely by accident, after scribbling lines on the back of a theme. The pleasure of discovering that he could write creatively motivated him to read poetry extensively and continue his own writing. He entered college hoping to become a poet. During his long undergraduate years, seventeen of his poems, some under various pseudonyms, appeared in the *Prairie Schooner* alone. Altogether, he published thirty-six poems before his graduation, some in prominent magazines. Bertrand Schultz recalls that even as an undergraduate Eiseley was known as "the poet laureate of the University of Nebraska." His greatest thrill, though, was "to receive a check from *Poetry: A Magazine of Verse* with an accompanying note, in her own hand, from Harriet Monroe."[7]

Eiseley's earliest poems appeared in the *Freshman Scrapbook* supplement to the *Prairie Schooner* in its third issue, published in July, 1927. There Loren placed a group of three five-line lyrics entitled "Cinquains," and his first narrative poem, "There is no Peace." The longer poem is noteworthy for its early treatment of what were to become major themes for Eiseley—blizzards, cold, desolation, ice, and death. Most of all it reveals his desperate state of mind after his father's death.

Many of the undergraduate poems are of course conventional lyrics on loss, extinction, death, the illusion of love, and the brevity of time—

"graveyard poems" as a college friend once called them. They display a reasonable mastery of standard poetic forms but no exceptional promise of future talent. Notable chiefly for their sustained pessimism and melancholy mood, few achieve real pathos or eloquence.

Perhaps Eiseley's best early verse was a series of four poems entitled "Bleak Uplands," published in the April, 1930, issue of *Voices*.[8] In these four ballads and sonnets—"Against Lineage," "Upland Harvest," "Words to the Stoic," and "Be Glad, You Worshippers"—Loren pictured the struggle between man and nature to claim the prairie. Despite man's efforts to keep the land under tillage, weeds would finally have their way as the land returned to fallow. Eiseley reveals his atavistic bent, his sympathy with natural processes that thwart "the prayers of men for fertile ground." The farmer who plows these fields must be a stoic to give thanks for even the "failing harvest and the meagre food." Despite their pastoral imagery, these poems deny the possibility of harmony between man and nature. Nature on the Great Plains, unpredictable and destructive, will not be tamed for man's benefit. In another ironic pastoral, "The Poet Surveys His Garden," the narrator wryly indulges the insects which ravage his garden. A related poem, "Tasker's Farm," describes the human cost of settling the prairie through the story of a young farm wife who runs away with a stranger to escape a stingy husband and her bleak life. However perversely, his poems side with the natural processes that frustrate man's attempts to establish homesteads on the open prairie. Many of these poems suggest an inhuman perspective not unlike that of Robinson Jeffers, a poet Eiseley much admired.

The Influence of Robinson Jeffers

During his graduate study, Eiseley remained active as a poet and reviewer, publishing up to a dozen poems a year in various small literary magazines. As time permitted, he kept in touch with old friends from the *Prairie Schooner*. In a letter to Lowry Wimberly, he mentions meeting Harold Vinal, a wealthy New Yorker who edited and published *Voices*.[9] Eiseley had contributed poems and reviews to *Voices* since 1930, and had often corresponded with Vinal, who sent him books for review and poems of his own to be appraised or to be considered for the *Prairie Schooner*.

From 1931 to 1935, Eiseley wrote five poetry reviews for *Voices* that helped define his own sensibility. These reviews show his distaste for modernists and his preference for more traditional, even romantic poets: George Dillon, Edgar Lee Masters, Edna St. Vincent Millay, Lord Dunsany, Lew Sarett, Edward Weismiller, Jesse Stuart, and Robinson Jeffers. On a trip to California in the early 1930s Eiseley had met and conversed with Jeffers on the road beyond "Tor House."[10] Later Jeffers wrote to thank Eiseley for the review, "Music of the Mountain," which had recently appeared in *Voices.*

In this review, Eiseley values those elements in Jeffers's work akin to his own spirit.[11] The inspiration Jeffers found in the rugged Carmel coast, like that Thoreau found at Walden, was a "rare phenomenon." It represented, in Eiseley's words, "the complete identification of the individual with his environment, or, rather, the extension of the environment into the individual to such a degree that the latter seems almost a lens, a gathering point through which, in some psychic and unexplainable manner, is projected a portion of the diversified and terrific forces of nature that otherwise stream helplessly away without significance to humanity." Drawn as he was to the Nebraska prairie and Badlands, Eiseley could appreciate the way Jeffers's poetry reflected the Pacific coastline below Tor House.

Eiseley especially admired Jeffers's attempt to combine fact and imagination in his approach to nature. "It is a simple thing to see a rock with the eyes," he observes, "less simple to see it with the heart." In Jeffers Eiseley found "the poet of the new science, the interpreter of our age"—comments later applied to himself. The implicit mysticism of Jeffers's "cosmic order of nature" reinforced Eiseley's sensibility. With disdain for cities and technology, Jeffers "wasted no time eulogizing machinery and buildings that will be outmoded tomorrow." He measured their impermanence against the timeless beauty of the natural world; his pessimism reflected "man's dismay before the conclusions of modern science." Nor did Jeffers's "inhumanism" bother Eiseley. On the contrary, in his austere loneliness "there is greater pride of life than in the words of many optimists."

Eiseley tempered Jeffers's "inhumanism" with gentle misanthropy; he feared man's transience but did not desire his extinction. Both men placed their hopes in the vitality of nature. Each sought to empathize with the creatures of the wild—particularly with the raptors and predators they so admired. Nature was for each the norm against which man is measured, but Eiseley was also troubled by something remote and cold in Jeffers's sensibility. In "Stature Against the Earth," Eiseley was put off by the unrelieved tragedy of *Give Your Heart to the Hawks,* and observed that "men are uneasy in the company of the gods."[12] He wished for some future Jeffers volume "in which madness and the dread weight of the cosmos might be laid aside in favor of some slower, less important, life-loving theme, that would give his zest for the land full scope."

Though he shared with Jeffers a romantic primitivism and a love for wild, remote settings, Eiseley's early poetry still reflects more of his compassion for life and less of the pain and cruelty, the agony of spirit prevalent in Jeffers's work. Eiseley also drew more upon paleontological or archeological material for his poems, rather than creating his own personal mythology, as did Jeffers. Despite these differences, however, both doubted the unqualified benefits of science and technology.

All the Night Wings

All the Night Wings is a rather uneven volume, including both Eiseley's earliest and last poetry. The first sixty-odd titles were assembled from various literary magazines where they appeared over a twenty-year period, while the last fourteen pieces are miscellaneous selections that he chose not to include in *Another Kind of Autumn*. Though published posthumously as Eiseley's last poetry volume, the major part of the book represents a wide though not definitive collection of his early poetry. Together with the selections from *The Star Thrower,* they illustrate the kind of poetry he was writing from 1928 to 1945. Some of the poems were originally intended for a volume Eiseley once planned to publish entitled *Fox Curse.* [13] The title chosen by editor Kenneth Heuer comes from a late poem, "All the Night Wings," since Eiseley customarily entitled his poetry volumes after the poem that best expressed the theme or mood of the collection. In this case the title poem evokes a nocturnal world of moths, owls, and flying squirrels—a melancholy, autumnal world of drifting leaves, graveyards, and death.

What is perhaps most striking about this fourth and largest collection of Eiseley's poetry is its unrelieved gloom and the virtual absence of persons besides the speaker. Aside from one selection, "Road Night Remembered," recalling his hobo experiences, and another, "Tasker's Farm," about a runaway farm wife, the poetry is almost entirely self-absorbed. Aside from occasional laments to an unnamed lover, the poems present a bleak, autumnal world of coyotes, foxes, spiders, hawks, and bats—images that become metaphors evoking moods of loneliness and loss. The world of Eiseley's early poems is a flat, monochromatic landscape, a night world of decay and death with rarely a spring poem; even more rarely is there a poem about any human joy or happiness.

Many of these poems are frankly adolescent in tone and subject matter, preoccupied with Eiseley's own emotional life. The sensibility they reveal is moody and immature, given to frequent expressions of loneliness and self-pity. His treatment of death is often downright morbid, as in the "Sonnets for a Second Death." Eiseley clearly needed the discipline of writing about something other than himself—of finding an "objective correlative" for his emotions. His early animal poems are perhaps his best efforts, suggesting that his instinct to collect them in the volume entitled *Fox Curse* was a sound one. When he could project himself into the body of a fox or wolf, as in "Song of the Wolf's Coat," "Coyote Country," or "Fox Curse," he wrote some memorable animistic poetry that evokes the lonely sweep of the prairie. Others poems, however, seem like conventional expressions of the "storm and stress" of prolonged adolescence, with more posturing as the poet than real poetic achievement.

Two later sonnets strike a quieter, though still artificially "Keatsian" note. "Now in This Drowsy Moment" and "October Has the Heart" show the power of his subdued lyricism, despite their lack of originality. Like the dreamy Frost of *A Boy's Will,* Eiseley still had to outgrow romantic posturing and diction before he could attain his true poetic voice, which he eventually found through the familiar essay as Frost had found it through the dramatic monologue. Unfortunately, few selections in *All the Night Wings* represent Eiseley's poetry at its best. His poetic maturity would not arrive until *Another Kind of Autumn.* Here, in his archeological poems, voice and vision were to find appropriate subject matter in a detached, scholarly treatment of time.

Notes of an Alchemist

When Eiseley returned to poetry in the 1960s, his turbulent early years had settled into a quiet domestic life and wide professional recognition. While hints of stress still appear in some autobiographical poems, the verse is generally more measured and subdued. After 1964 he began publishing a few poems a year in popular and scholarly magazines. Some of these transitional pieces were never afterward collected, but most found their way into the three volumes of poetry Eiseley published before his death. By 1972, he had accumulated enough verse that his editor at Scribner's, Kenneth Heuer, proposed a poetry volume. That volume became *Notes of an Alchemist,* which provoked only mild surprise from reviewers who had suspected his poetic abilities.

Notes of an Alchemist is a curiously tentative volume, as its title suggests. In his disarming preface Eiseley pretends to offer random jottings of a lifetime's scientific study—the "alchemy" by which "a scientific man has transmuted for his personal pleasure the sharp images of his profession into something deeply subjective." What the preface fails to mention is that Eiseley had cherished a long ambition as a poet, having already published more than seventy poems earlier in life. His tone suggests a wary belletrist hoping to deflect the bolts of criticism from his work by pretending to disinterested amateurism. It was one of the ruses of the fox.

As the title implies, *Notes of an Alchemist* is a volume of transmutations: from experience to memory to poetry—base elements to gold—by means of reenactment through memory. In the title poem, the mind is compared to the recesses of a subterranean cave, where crystals of strange shapes and colors grow. Composing a poem is likened to the slow growth of a crystal in the recesses of the mind. Two other meditations on the nature of poetry, "The Hand Ax" and "Think That I Spoke to You," continue this theme. Words, like broken artifacts, shift and erode in the torrents of time, despite efforts to fix their meaning. They erode far more quickly than the rough stone ax that Eiseley handles, though his poems are fabricated with as much loving care. Poetry is both "the art of the ephemeral" and "the art of the continually renewed or always present," he reflects in "Think That I Spoke to You." It is a voice gesture, a cry lost in the wind.

Eiseley's "transmutations" are momentary extensions of vision recorded in free verse. Like his mentor, Frank Speck, Eiseley ceased to "study" the primitive mindset and came to enter into it and fully accept magic, shamanism, and animism as a coherent account of the mysteries in the natural world which science failed to explain. A poem in his second volume, "In the Red Sunset on Another Hill," perhaps best explains this curiously arcane vision, as well as recapitulating the transmutation theme and the dominant images from *Notes of an Alchemist*. Eiseley's conversion to alchemy took place many years ago as he was fossil-hunting in the Badlands.

What these poems present are the emotional associations Eiseley accumulated over many years as a scientist but could not express within the language of his profession: the paleontologist's fascination in "conjuring up" extinct forms of life through his careful fossil reconstructions; the archeologist's fey sense of reencountering the past upon finding a pharoah's funeral "toys" in a pyramid; the anthropologist's feeling of kinship with the cultures he studies; or the evolutionist's vision of extinct forms of life shifting through time as before his eyes.

In primitive magic, poetry and science find their common origin. Magic, after all, is the precursor of science as Karl Popper has shown; it provided primitive man with a coherent framework for understanding and attempting to control the natural world. So, too, the roots of poetry trace back to primitive chant and incantation. What Eiseley attempts to find is a new "mythos," a means of articulating what lies beyond the realm of science. This new poetic mythos would be based on Native American ethnology and anthropology. Though Eiseley had a romantic sensibility, he found he could no longer write in the manner of the romantic poets. Conventional literary models were inadequate to write about nature, and classical and British conventions of pastoral poetry had exhausted themselves: Pan and his nymphs and dryads had no place in the New World, particularly not on the Great Plains. But Eiseley could draw upon a wealth of American Indian myths, customs, and beliefs to express his sense of the mystery of nature.

Nor could the idiom of science express his sense of awe and wonder. In "Five Men from the Great Sciences" he parts company with the conventional scientific point of view that seeks to understand nature from outside of nature. His desire is to return to the "within"; to merge himself with the forces of life that can only be comprehended intuitively, poetically. Objective understanding alone is inadequate: obsessed with measuring and recording, we no longer recognize things for what they are. There are other, more ancient ways of knowing, he intimates, that we have forgotten in our obsession with facts. So he forsakes the world of science for the primitive world of Game Lords, Tricksters, Shape-shifters, Druids, wizards, sorcerers, and magicians. Through his poetry he actively empathizes and merges himself with what in the past he had only studied: running with the snow leopard, leaping with the gar, soaring with the condor, and laughing with the "old ones." But is this simply mystification and obscurity—or the expression of a new poetic mythos? In the poem "Magic" Eiseley explores these issues. Magic, according to Malinowski, "simply was from the beginning"; it is a response to life's uncertainties. Later in the poem, Eiseley explains: "Magic runs to the beginnings of life because / life is a gift and uncertain." This rather sophisticated sense of "magic" clarifies what Eiseley meant in his autobiography when he remarked, "I have come to believe that in the world there is nothing to explain the world"; certainly not the metaphysics of science. Thus poetry permitted Eiseley to carry his speculations beyond the realm of the essay, using the logic of association, of meditative free verse, to express what he felt most deeply about his personal world.

The Innocent Assassins

Heartened by the response to *Notes of an Alchemist* in 1972, Eiseley assembled a second volume of poetry the following year to pursue these same speculations. *The Innocent Assassins* is in many respects a companion volume, with little difference in theme or focus. The topics are still diverse—autobiography, ethnology, natural history, and prehistory. As implied in the title poem, "The Innocent Assassins," and the dedication, this volume draws on experiences from his bone-hunting days, but is not limited to them. Paleontology provides a framework for Eiseley's speculations in this volume, as archeology does in his next volume, *Another Kind of Autumn*. He ponders the mystery of extinction in the natural order, as he subsequently would write about the disappearance of human civilizations. The poems in *The Innocent Assassins* probe the human significance of paleontology and explore the meaning of the vast fossil record that man has accumulated. Does this natural history of life have any intrinsic message, besides satisfying man's curiosity about the past? Eiseley's poetic instincts hunger for direction or purpose, even in the form of shamanistic magic, though his scientific sensibility accepts the futility of teleological questions. Life poses only questions, not answers. The cryptic message he finds in "That Vast Thing Sleeping" is the inevitable life cycle of most species:

> tiny to large, then gone. Six syllables that tell
> time's stairway ends upon a rail-less balcony
> for all of life.

All the typical Eiseley concerns are in this poem: man's roots in evolution and the oblivion toward which he is headed, sooner or later.

The muse for this volume is *Mu,* the primeval voice of chaos. Eiseley envisions the natural order as a "rope" of numberless forms drawn from chaos only to return there eventually. Nature is a great charnel house of extinct forms that no sorcerer or magician can reanimate, so Eiseley evokes a personal myth of preexistence in order to probe life's origins. "I grasp all that went before," he announces in one poem, and "I have borne much to reach this thing, myself" in another. He dreams the ultimate atavistic dream: to revert to simpler, prehuman, preconscious forms of life. He hungers for the "innocence" of the world as it existed before man, but will as he might, he cannot cast thought in nonhuman shape. The very title of the volume betrays the anthropocentrism he wishes to escape.

From the evolutionary perspective of these poems, contemporary man and his vast technology dwindle to insignificance. Measured against the duration of time and the power of natural forces, his efforts to master nature seem puny and ephemeral. Perhaps this theme of human insignificance unifies the diverse material in *The Innocent Assassins* and indicates the direction Eiseley's poetry would take in his final volume, *Another Kind of Autumn*. [14]

Another Kind of Autumn

Thoreau once wrote that civilizations are like toadstools springing up in the night. This sense of the transience of human civilizations marks Eiseley's last book of poetry, *Another Kind of Autumn*. The title itself implies the dominant metaphor in this volume about the "autumn" of great civilizations: their decline and fall. This archeological metaphor shapes Eiseley's poetic musings about the reasons for the extinction of past civilizations: Egyptian, Minoan, Mayan, and Sumerian. *Another Kind of Autumn* is perhaps his most successful book of verse because vision and voice are unified by themes—the contemplation of archeological artifacts and ruins—not so remote as to deny human perspective. Nor is there any evidence of the misanthropic bitterness or moralizing that mars some poems in his previous works. Here his voice speaks most naturally and unassumingly, without portentousness. Time is presented on a human scale, without mention of the vast epochs of prehuman life.

Eiseley views civilizations as organic entities, each with its own birth, development, maturity, and decay. The poems in *Another Kind of Autumn* may be read as a series of glosses on this theme. But unlike living creatures, great cultures have no self-regulating mechanisms, so their only destiny is to spread, produce seeds, and replant themselves somewhere else before they die. The final measure of a civilization, then, is its duration rather than its power. In *The Invisible Pyramid,* Eiseley praises poets for their "preternatural sensitivity to the backward and forward reaches of time," comments that could just as easily be applied to himself. He is the "time-voyager" who returns from the past with the "unbearably sad song" of man's attempts to efface time. Autumn in this poetry volume becomes the time of civilizations' decline: the individual poems are verbal artifacts, the recording of their passing.

One might almost think of Eiseley's poems as abstracts of his familiar essays—brief summations of ideas stripped of their rich texture of allusion and reduced to images or impressions in discursive free verse. The poems are analogous to journal entries: they are in fact verse notes of a continuous verse journal, comprised of deliberately unfinished poems. Hence the wide variety of topics that reappear in each volume. *Another Kind of Autumn* includes, besides the archeological poems, verse on the migration of hawks, falcons, and monarch butterflies, the Viking Mars space probe, a Victorian dollhouse, a bittern, cacti, deer, and Sphex wasps—more natural history and fewer autobiographical poems than in the previous two volumes. The tone of the entire volume is elegiac, reflecting the fact that it was completed during the last few months of Eiseley's final illness.

Nevertheless, it also reflects his prophetic sense as an evolutionist that our technological civilization will decline like the great cultures of the past.

Eiseley's poems are troublesome to the reader because they are so tentative, so unsure of what they accomplish. Even after he moved from lyric to discursive poetry, his verse still too often seems belabored. Yet the best of Eiseley's poems capture and hold a passing moment of time, whether it be the accomplishment of a dead civilization, the moment of a volcano's eruption in ancient Crete, or the discovery of funeral toys in a pharoah's tomb. The poems project the quality of overheard thoughts or ruminations, verse meditations spoken gravely and solemnly aloud. What they lack is the humor or irony of a poetic voice less portentous and self-important. After all, the prevailing voice in most contemporary poetry is much less stiff and formal than this—more often brash or colloquial. Too often Eiseley sounds like the scientist rather than the poet in his verse, despite its discursive format. The formal voice and the informal poetic structure seem at odds with one another.

Though Eiseley's poetry volumes have sold well, he has yet to establish his poetic standing as securely as his prose reputation. He matured as a poet so late in his career that his poetry was only available during the last ten years of his life—not enough time to gain adequate critical recognition. The specialized subject matter of many poems may also discourage the nonscientific reader. Despite the praise of Auden and Nemerov, Eiseley's poetry still needs to find a wider academic audience before it will earn the kind of careful critical attention it deserves. Whether his poems will gain a firm place in contemporary American verse, or remain a footnote to Eiseley's eloquent books and essays, is yet to be determined.

Conclusion

From anthropologist to essayist to poet, Eiseley's literary journey was indeed an immense one. He had the good fortune to live during the period after World War II when science established its preeminence in America, and when its authority was undisputed. But he was also farsighted enough to anticipate the problems that would arise from unquestioning faith in a technological vision of the future, and he spoke eloquently of these doubts in his most memorable essays. His reputation would have been established alone by his revitalizing the familiar essay, even if he had not written his acclaimed autobiography and his extensive poetry. Perhaps more than anyone else Eiseley is responsible for originating the style of the current popular scientific idiom practiced by Lewis Thomas, Carl Sagan, Robert

Jastrow, Stephen Jay Gould, and others. And if there is a movement among scientists today to reassert the humane values that are intrinsic to science wisely practiced,then credit for that must also be due in part to Eiseley.

His accomplishments are so numerous—as scientist, teacher, administrator, lecturer, historian of science, naturalist, essayist, and poet—that it is difficult to predict what shape his reputation will take. But suffice it to say that his style of supple, lyrical prose remains his foremost accomplishment. It is certain that Eiseley will be read alongside Montaigne, Bacon, Lamb, Hazlitt, and Thoreau as one of the great masters of the familiar essay. The voice in his essays spoke "not of an age but for all time."

Notes and References

Chapter One

1. Schultz offered this assessment at "The Loren C. Eiseley Memorial Convocation" on November 28, 1977, at the University of Nebraska–Lincoln.
2. These comments appear in Eiseley's autobiographical essay "The Mind as Nature," in *The Night Country* (New York, 1971), p. 196.
3. Ibid., pp. 195–96.
4. Caroline E. Werkley, "Report of Loren Eiseley Collection/July, 1978," manuscript, p. 7, in University of Pennsylvania Archives.
5. Charles Kingsley, *Water Babies* (New York: Macmillan Co., 1907), pp. 69–71.
6. The holograph manuscript of this early unpublished juvenilia is in the Loren Eiseley Collection at the University of Pennsylvania.
7. As quoted by Caroline Werkley in "Report of Loren Eiseley Collection/ July, 1978," p. 26.
8. Bob Lancaster recounts this story in "Loren Eiseley's Immense Journey," *Today/The Philadelphia Inquirer,* January 27, 1974, p. 18.
9. As mentioned by Rudolph Umland, letter to the author, July 31, 1979.
10. Rudolph Umland, "Looking Back at the Wimberly Years," manuscript.
11. This essay was first published as "Endure the Night" in the *Atlantic Monthly,* June, 1963, pp. 75–78 and has also been anthologized under this title elsewhere.
12. Paul B. Sears included this anecdote in his remarks at "The Loren C. Eiseley Memorial Service" at the University of Pennsylvania on November 7, 1977; the manuscript is in the University of Pennsylvania Archives.
13. Umland, "Looking Back at the Wimberly Years."
14. "Autumn—A Memory," *Prairie Schooner* 1, no. 4 (October, 1927): 238–39.
15. For additional discussion of Wimberly's editorship of the *Prairie Schooner,* see Rudolph Umland's "Lowry Wimberly of the *Prairie Schooner*: His Magazine Put Nebraska on Literary Map," *Kansas City Star,* July 30, 1964, and his "Lowry Wimberly and Others: Recollections of a Beer Drinker," *Prairie Schooner* 51, no. 1 (Spring, 1977): 17–51.
16. Dr. Bertrand Schultz has offered these reminiscences about his undergraduate friendship with Eiseley and their work together on the South Party in

the tribute he prepared for the "Loren C. Eiseley Memorial Service" at the University of Pennsylvania on November 7, 1977.

17. This conservative estimate of early man's antiquity in North America prevailed among some anthropologists until after World War II.

18. This letter is reprinted courtesy of Wilbur Gaffney and the Estate of Loren C. Eiseley.

19. Eiseley sometimes dated this story in 1927 or 1928, although it was actually first published in the *Prairie Schooner* 9, no. 1 (Winter, 1935):33–39.

20. Some of the material that Eiseley prepared for "They Hunted the Mammoth" may later have been included in at least ten professional and popular articles that he published between 1942 and 1947.

21. Schultz's account is of course more direct and factual. The reporters' dialogue, the account of Buzby's "petrified woman," and the character of Mullens are probably fictionalized in Loren's version of the discovery of the fossil quarry.

22. The two papers which Eiseley coauthored with Frank Speck are "Significance of Hunting Territory Systems of the Algonkian in Social Theory," *American Anthropologist* 41, no. 2 (April–June, 1939):269–80; and "Montagnais-Naskapi Bands and Family Hunting Districts of the Central and Southeastern Labrador Peninsula," *American Philosophical Society Proceedings* 85, no. 2 (January, 1942):215–42.

23. Eiseley later extensively revised each of these articles. "Obituary of a Bone Hunter" first appeared in *Harper's,* October, 1947, pp. 325–29; "Buzby's Petrified Woman," *Harper's,* November, 1948, pp. 76–79; and "People Leave Skulls With Me," *Harper's,* May, 1951, pp. 43–49.

24. Eiseley eventually coauthored two articles with Schultz, "Paleontological Evidence for the Antiquity of the Scottsbluff Bison Quarry and Its Associated Artifacts," *American Anthropologist* 37, no. 2 (April–June, 1935):306–19; and "An Added Note on the Scottsbluff Quarry," *American Anthropologist* 38, no. 3 (July–September, 1936):521–24.

25. Rudolph Umland, "Lowry Wimberly and Others: Recollections of a Beerdrinker," *Prairie Schooner* 51, no. 1 (Spring, 1977):29.

26. *Nebraska: A Guide to the Cornhusker State* (New York: Viking Press, 1939), p. 143.

27. "Three Indices of Quaternary Time and Their Bearing on the Problem of American Prehistory: A Critique," Ph.D. diss., University of Pennsylvania, 1937.

28. "Index Mollusca and Their Bearing on Certain Problems of Prehistory: A Critique," *Twenty-Fifth Anniversary Series of the Philadelphia Anthropological Society* (Philadelphia: University of Pennsylvania, 1937), pp. 71–92.

29. The Folsom Culture refers to late Pleistocene man in North America. It is named for the beautifully wrought stone points found in conjunction with the remains of extinct mammals by scientists at Folsom, New Mexico, in 1927. These may date early man in North America as early as 15–25,000 years ago. They were basically a primitive nomadic hunting culture.

Chapter Two

1. All of the chapters in *The Immense Journey* except for "The Slit" and "The Dream Animal" first appeared as magazine articles, some of them with slightly different titles.

2. The original titles Eiseley had considered for his book were "Man Hunt," "The Great Deeps," and "The Crack in the Absolute" before he found the phrase "the immense journey" in a quote from Amiel.

3. Eiseley's correspondence with editor John Fischer at Harper & Brothers provides a fascinating study in the genesis of *The Immense Journey*. In an August 9, 1956, letter Fischer explained why his firm had decided against publishing Eiseley's essays in book form. This correspondence can be found in the Eiseley Collection at the University of Pennsylvania Archives.

4. See Hiram Haydn's account of his professional acquaintance with Eiseley in his memoirs, *Words and Faces* (New York, 1974), pp. 102–3, 122–23, 281–85.

5. An excellent introductory discussion of *The Immense Journey* can be found in "Loren Eiseley," in *Gateway to the Great Books,* vol. 8, *Natural Science,* ed. Robert M. Hutchins and Mortimer J. Adler (Chicago: Encyclopedia Britannica, 1963), pp. 120–22.

6. Henri Bergson, *Creative Evolution* (New York: Random House, 1944), p. 109. Although Eiseley decided against using this epigraph in *The Immense Journey,* the influence of Bergson is still apparent throughout the book.

7. One of the most intemperate criticisms of Eiseley's style occurred in a review of *The Firmament of Time* by John Buettner-Janusch, who faulted Eiseley for his "sentimental and trite" writing, his "fevered prose, overblown metaphor, and sentimental twaddle." See the *American Anthropologist* 65, no. 3, pt. 1 (June, 1963):9.

8. Two of Eiseley's best discussions of the difference between natural history and science can be found in "The Enchanted Glass," *American Scholar* 26, no. 478 (Fall, 1957):478–92 and chapter 9 of *The Night Country,* "Strangeness in the Proportion." For further reading, see Joseph Wood Krutch's introduction to the genre of the natural history essay in his lengthy prologue to *Great American Nature Writing* (New York: William Sloane, 1950).

9. These remarks may be found in a May 2, 1966, letter from Eiseley to Dr. Edwin G. Boring of Harvard (in the Eiseley Collection, University of Pennsylvania Archives). Eiseley was director for a time of the Richard Prentice Ettinger Program for Creative Writing (in the sciences) at the Rockefeller Institute in New York.

10. C. P. Snow's *The Two Cultures and the Scientific Revolution* (New York: Cambridge University Press, 1959) contains one of the earliest and best discussions of the cultural and intellectual division between the humanities and the sciences. Eiseley dismisses this gap, however, as more imagined than real in "The Illusion of the Two Cultures," *American Scholar* 33, no. 3 (Summer, 1964):387–99 and later reprinted in *The Star Thrower.*

11. Thomas H. Huxley, *On a Piece of Chalk* (New York: Charles Scribner's Sons, 1967).

12. Edmund Fuller, ed., *The Great English and American Essays* (New York: Avon Books, 1964), p. 9.

13. The surprisingly few critical essays dealing with Eiseley's work are reflected in the bibliographic entries for this study. Aside from E. Fred Carlisle's two articles and James Schwartz's piece, there are only a small number of "appreciations" and several dissertations.

14. Van Wyck Brooks, *In the Shadow of the Mountain: My Post-Meridian Years* (New York: E. P. Dutton & Co., 1961), p. 21.

15. Eiseley opened the "Adventures of the Mind" series with "An Evolutionist Looks at Modern Man," *Saturday Evening Post,* April 26, 1958, pp. 26, 120–25. His television series, "Animal Secrets," won the 1966 Thomas Alva Edison Foundation National Mass Media Award for "best science television program for youth," and a "special citation in recognition of its contribution to public education in science" from the National Science Teachers Association.

Chapter Three

1. A full discussion of Eiseley's involvement with Barlow's firm may be found in Caroline E. Werkley's "The Old Bones Man: Report of the Barlow File," manuscript, University of Pennsylvania Archives.

2. These papers were "The Program on the Darwin Collection in the Library" and "The Reception of the First Missing Links," *Proceedings of the American Philosophical Society* 98, no. 6 (December 23, 1954):449–52, 453–65. The third and most important article was "Charles Darwin, Edward Blyth, and the Theory of Natural Selection," *Proceedings of the American Philosophical Society* 103, no. 1 (February 28, 1959):94–158.

3. Actually, Wallace's essay, "On the Tendency of Varieties to Depart Indefinitely from the Original Type," was read along with an excerpt from Darwin's unpublished manuscript of 1844; and both were published in the *Journal of the Proceedings of the Linnean Society,* 1858, p. 45.

4. Originally published as "The Ethic of the Group" in *Social Control in a Free Society,* ed. Robert Spiller (Philadelphia: University of Pennsylvania Press, 1960), pp. 15–38.

5. This chapter was originally published as "Nature, Man, and Miracle" in *Horizon* 11, no. 6 (July, 1960):25–32.

6. Stephen Jay Gould evaluates Eiseley's theory in the context of recent Darwin scholarship in his review, "Darwin Vindicated!" *New York Review of Books,* August 16, 1979, pp. 36–38.

7. As mentioned in Howard E. Gruber's review, "The Origin of the *Origin of Species,*" *New York Times Book Review,* July 22, 1979, pp. 7, 16.

8. Gould, "Darwin Vindicated!" p. 38.

9. "The Program on the Darwin Collection in the Library," *Proceedings of the American Philosophical Society* 98, no. 6 (December 23, 1954):451–52.

Chapter Four

1. Caroline E. Werkley, "Report of Loren Eiseley Collection/Revised, September, 1978," p. 46, manuscript, University of Pennsylvania Archives.
2. Also published in *Science,* April 21, 1961, pp. 1197–1201.
3. May 19, 1962, pp. 68–71.
4. The entire record of this correspondence between Eiseley and the University of Nebraska Press can be found in the University of Pennsylvania Archives.
5. See Basil Willey's discussion in "Bacon and the Rehabilitation of Science," in *The Seventeenth Century Background* (New York: Columbia University Press, 1960), pp. 24–40.
6. Review by Theodosius Dobzhansky, *American Anthropologist* 73 (1971):305–6.
7. W. H. Auden, "Concerning the Unpredictable," *New Yorker,* February 21, 1970, pp. 118–25. Auden's essay also appears as the Introduction to *The Star Thrower,* pp. 19–20.
8. As quoted from a July 6, 1970, letter to W. H. Frey in the University of Pennsylvania Archives.
9. As found in a 1971 letter to Curtis Cate, Saint Exupery's biographer, in the University of Pennsylvania Archives.
10. Eiseley had planned five divisions for the book: (1) science and humanism; (2) poems 1930–40; (3) nature; (4) poems 1950–76; (5) silhouettes of autobiography. (University of Pennsylvania Archives.)
11. Heuer omits a slight criticism that Auden originally made on the first page of his review when it appeared in *New Yorker.* See "Concerning the Unpredictable," *New Yorker,* February 21, 1970, p. 118.
12. As expressed in an August 30, 1973, letter to Professor Walter G. Harding, in the University of Pennsylvania Archives.
13. Michael G. Cooke uses this phrase in a review of *All the Strange Hours*: "The Hero in Autobiography," *Yale Review* 65, no. 4 (June, 1976):592.
14. *New York Times,* November 6, 1972, p. 41.

Chapter Five

1. Loren Eiseley Collection, University of Pennsylvania Archives.
2. James Olney, *"All the Strange Hours,"* *New Republic,* November 1, 1975, p. 31.
3. Heywood Hale Broun, "A Conversation with Loren Eiseley," Avid Reader Audio Cassettes, no. 40218 (New York: Jeffrey Norton Publishers, 1975).
4. The lecture was subsequently published as *The Mind as Nature,* Foreword by Arthur G. Wirth (New York, 1962).
5. Loren Eiseley Collection, University of Pennsylvania Archives.
6. "The Divine Animal" was used as the title for his Blashfield Address to the American Academy of Arts and Letters, however. "The Uncompleted Man" was the original title for chapter 4.

7. Loren Eiseley Collection, University of Pennsylvania Archives.

8. As inspired by W. J. Locke's *The Golden Journey of Mr. Paradyne* (New York: Dodd, Mead and Co., 1924). See also discussion in chapter 1.

9. The original version of this essay, *Man, Time, and Prophecy,* was published as a limited edition Christmas gift book by Harcourt, Brace & World in 1966.

10. Cf. "Activism and the Rejection of History," *Science,* July 11, 1969, p. 129; and Eiseley's introduction to *The Shape of Likelihood: Relevance and the University,* Preface by Taylor Littleton (University: University of Alabama Press, 1971), pp. 3–18. See also the poem "Confrontation" in *Notes of an Alchemist,* pp. 98–99.

11. Caroline E. Werkley describes this curious episode in "Professor Cope, Not Alive But Well," *Smithsonian* 6 (August, 1975):72–75.

12. Eiseley was given this award by the Nebraska Society of Washington, D.C.

13. See Kenneth Heuer's "Editor's Preface" to *The Star Thrower,* p. 12.

14. Loren Eiseley Collection, University of Pennsylvania Archives.

15. University of Pennsylvania Archives.

16. James Olney's *"All the Strange Hours,"* *New Republic,* November 1, 1975, pp. 30–34 is perhaps the most perceptive review of Eiseley's autobiography.

17. Loren Eiseley Collection, University of Pennsylvania Archives.

18. Ibid.

19. In the final version of the book, Eiseley omitted a last chapter, "Beyond the Curtain" (chapter 26) and substantially revised others.

20. See John N. Morris's excellent theoretical discussion of autobiography in the "Introduction" to *Versions of the Self* (New York: Basic Books, 1966), p. 11. See also James Olney, *Metaphors of Self: The Meaning of Autobiography* (Princeton: Princeton University Press, 1972) and Roy Pascal, *Design and Truth in Autobiography* (Cambridge: Harvard University Press, 1960).

21. As Eiseley remarked in his interview with Heywood Hale Broun. See note 3 above.

22. This speech was given in Fort Worth, Texas, in June, 1974.

Chapter Six

1. During this time he wrote more than one hundred collected and uncollected poems, and at least ten poetry and book reviews.

2. E. Fred Carlisle, "The Poetic Achievement of Loren Eiseley," *Prairie Schooner* 51, no. 2 (Summer, 1977):112.

3. Two of Eiseley's late poems that appeared in the *American Scholar,* "The Hawk," and "Epitaph," were never collected, and there may well be others.

4. Auden dedicated "Unpredictable But Providential" to Eiseley, the poem first appearing in the *New Yorker,* April 14, 1973, p. 40, and later in *Thank You,*

Fog (New York: Random House, 1974), pp. 9–10; Nemerov dedicated "The Rent in the Screen" to him, the poem appearing in *Gnomes & Occasions* (Chicago: University of Chicago Press, 1973), p. 64.

5. As quoted in the "Foreword" to *All the Night Wings,* p. xii.

6. Ben Howard's review of *The Innocent Assassins* in *Poetry* 126 (April, 1975): 44–46; and Daniel Hoffman's review of *Notes of an Alchemist,* "Eiseley Plumbs Unexpected Truths," *Sunday Bulletin Books* (Philadelphia), November 26, 1972, sec. 5, p. 7 are among the few reviews that show any real critical perception.

7. As mentioned by Caroline E. Werkley in "Report of Loren Eiseley Collection/Revised, September, 1978," p. 16.

8. "Bleak Uplands," *Voices* 55 (April, 1930):158–60.

9. As quoted in a November 14, 1933, letter from Eiseley to Wimberly in the University of Nebraska–Lincoln Archives, *Prairie Schooner* editor's correspondence. Vinal published *Voices: An Open Forum for Poets* from 1921 to 1965.

10. As Eiseley later recalled in his "Foreword" to *Not Man Apart: Lines from Robinson Jeffers,* ed. David Brower (San Francisco: Sierra Books, 1965), p. [1].

11. *Voices* 67 (December–January, 1932–33):42–47.

12. *Voices* 75 (April–May, 1934):53–56.

13. As mentioned in the "Foreword" to *All the Night Wings,* p. xiii.

14. Ben Howard identified this as one of the major themes in *The Innocent Assassins* in "Comment," *Poetry* 126 (April, 1975):44.

Selected Bibliography

PRIMARY SOURCES

1. Books

All the Night Wings. New York: Times Books, 1979. Poetry.

All the Strange Hours: An Excavation of a Life. New York: Charles Scribner's Sons, 1975. Autobiography.

Another Kind of Autumn. New York: Charles Scribner's Sons, 1977. Poetry.

The Brown Wasps: A Collection of Three Essays in Autobiography. Mt. Horeb, Wis.: Perishable Press, 1969. Includes "The Brown Wasps," "Big Eyes and Little Eyes," and "Endure the Night."

Darwin and the Mysterious Mr. X: New Light on the Evolutionists. New York: E. P. Dutton, 1979.

Darwin's Century: Evolution and the Men Who Discovered It. New York: Doubleday & Co., 1958.

The Firmament of Time. New York: Atheneum Publishers, 1960.

Francis Bacon and the Modern Dilemma. Lincoln: University of Nebraska Press, 1962. Revised and expanded as *The Man Who Saw Through Time*, 1973.

The Immense Journey. New York: Random House, 1957.

The Innocent Assassins. New York: Charles Scribner's Sons, 1973. Poetry.

The Invisible Pyramid. New York: Charles Scribner's Sons, 1970.

Man, Time, and Prophecy. New York: Harcourt, Brace and World, 1966. Reprinted as "The Chresmologue" in *The Night Country*, 1971.

The Man Who Saw Through Time. New York: Charles Scribner's Sons, 1973. Revised and enlarged edition of *Francis Bacon and the Modern Dilemma*, 1962.

The Mind as Nature. New York: Harper & Row, 1962. Reprinted with the same title as chapter 13 of *The Night Country*, 1971.

The Night Country. New York: Charles Scribner's Sons, 1971.

Notes of an Alchemist. New York: Charles Scribner's Sons, 1972. Poetry.

The Star Thrower. New York: Times Books, 1978.

The Unexpected Universe. New York: Harcourt, Brace and World, 1969.

2. Scientific Articles and Popular Essays

Loren Eiseley was such a prolific writer in so many fields that a bibliography of this kind cannot hope to be complete. Since he published a wide variety of both scientific and literary essays, entries in both categories are simply listed alphabetically by title. And since these categories often overlap, no attempt has been made to separate them. Nor are they arranged chronologically, though there might have been some logic in doing so. One should simply keep in mind the progression of his career and note the gradual appearance of his familiar essays after 1945.

These citations are important because Eiseley usually assembled his books from previously published essays, which were then revised and adapted for their new context. The customary progression of his ideas was from speech, to essay, to book form. Moreover, he often reprinted short excerpts or entire chapters from his books concurrently with or immediately following a book's publication, so it is sometimes difficult to decide whether an essay title precedes or follows the book in which it also appears. For this reason excerpts are included in this section to illustrate his publishing habits.

For reasons of space, the listing of Eiseley's book reviews here is limited to his early literary reviews, although he was an active literary and scientific reviewer throughout his career. Of his numerous later reviews, only a few which take the form of extended essays are included. These are listed in this section as essays.

"Activism and the Rejection of History." *Science,* July 11, 1969, p. 129.

"Alfred Russel Wallace." *Scientific American,* February, 1959, pp. 70–84.

"An Added Note on the Scottsbluff Quarry." *American Anthropology* 38 (July, 1936):521–24. With C. Bertrand Schultz.

"Antiquity of Modern Man." *Scientific American,* July, 1948, pp. 16–19.

"Apes Almost Men." *Prairie Schooner* 18, no. 3 (Fall, 1944):170–76.

"Archeological Observations on the Problem of Post-Glacial Extinction." *American Antiquity* 8 (January, 1943):209–17.

"Big Eyes and Small Eyes." *Gentry* 20 (Fall, 1956):30–31, 124–27.

"The Bird and the Machine." *Harper's,* January, 1956, pp. 69–73. Reprinted in *Reader's Digest* 71 (December, 1957), pp. 127–29. Later reprinted as "There Came a Cry of Joy," *Reader's Digest* 110 (March, 1977), pp. 97–99. Also appeared as "A Sparrow Hawk's Guidance Along the Immense Journey," *Defenders,* October, 1976, pp. 300–3.

"The Brown Wasps." *Gentry* 21 (Winter, 1956–57):80–81, 146–47. Also appeared in *Pennsylvania Gazette* 70 (December, 1971):22–25.

"Buzby's Petrified Woman." *Harper's,* November, 1948, pp. 76–79.

"Centennial of Discovery of Neanderthal Man." *Science,* December 14, 1956, p. 1183. With William Louis Straus.

"Charles Darwin." *Scientific American,* February, 1956, pp. 62–72.

"Charles Darwin, Edward Blyth, and the Theory of Natural Selection." *Proceedings of the American Philosophical Society* 103, no. 1 (February 28, 1959):94–158. Also published as a monograph with the same title: Lancaster, Penn.: Lancaster Press, 1961.

"Charles Lyell." *Scientific American,* August, 1959, pp. 98–106.

"Chimps: The Apes That Ape Man." *New York Times Magazine,* September 21, 1958, pp. 53, 56, 58.

"The Christmas of the Talking Cat." *House and Garden,* December, 1972, pp. 60–61, 143.

"Coming of the Giant Wasps." *Audubon,* September, 1975, pp. 34–39. Also appears in *Defenders,* June, 1976, pp. 152–57.

"The Cosmic Orphan." *Saturday Review World,* February 23, 1974, pp. 16–19. Also appears in the *Propaedia* of *The Encyclopedia Britannica,* 15th ed., pp. 206–8.

"The Cosmic Prison." *Horizon,* Autumn, 1970, pp. 96–101.

"Creature from the Marsh." *Natural History,* October, 1971, pp. 24–34.

"The Dance of the Frogs." *Audubon,* May, 1978, pp. 73–77.

"Darwin, Coleridge, and the Theory of Unconscious Creation." *Daedalus* 94 (Summer, 1965):588–602.

"Did the Folsom Bison Survive in Canada?" *Science Monthly* 56 (May, 1943):468–72.

"The Divine Animal." *Proceedings of the American Academy of Arts and Letters,* 2d ser. 14 (1964):333–41.

"Each Person is Forever the Eye." *Creative Living* 6, no. 3 (Summer, 1977):7.

"Early Man in South and East Africa." *American Anthropology* 50 (January, 1948):11–17.

"Eloquent Valedictory From a Far Valley." *Life,* August 13, 1965, p. 10.

"The Elvish Art of Enchantment." *Horn Book* 41 (August, 1965):364–67.

"The Enchanted Glass." *American Scholar* 26 (Fall, 1957):478–92.

"Endure the Night." *Atlantic Monthly,* June, 1963, pp. 75–78.

"Evidences of a Pre-Ceramic Cultural Horizon in Smith County." *Kansas Science* 89 (March 10, 1939):221.

"An Evolutionist Looks at Modern Man." *Saturday Evening Post,* April 26, 1958, pp. 26–29, 120–25.

"An Extreme Case of Scaphocephaly from a Mound Burial Near Troy, Kansas." *Transactions of the Kansas Academy of Science* 47 (1944–45):241–55. With C. Willett Asling.

"Fire and the Fauna." *American Anthropology* 49 (October, 1947):678–80.

"The Fire Apes." *Harper's,* September, 1949, pp. 47–55. Reprinted in *Holiday,* March, 1962, p. 170. Abridged as "Man's Rivals Are Waiting," *Science Digest,* February, 1950, pp. 57–62.

"Fire-Drive and the Extinction of the Terminal Pleistocene Fauna." *American Anthropology* 48 (January, 1946):54–59.

"The Flow of the River." *American Scholar* 22, no. 4 (Autumn, 1953):451–58.

"The Folsom Mystery." *Scientific American,* December, 1942, pp. 260–61.

"Fossil Man." *Scientific American,* December, 1953, pp. 65–72.

"Fossil Man: A Personal Credo." *American Journal of Physical Anthropology* 10, no. 1 (March, 1952): 1–6.

"The Fox and the Anthropologist." *Reader's Digest,* November, 1978, pp. 136–37.

"Francis Bacon." *Horizon,* Winter, 1964, pp. 32–47.

"Francis Bacon as Educator." *Science,* April 21, 1961, pp. 1197–1201. Reprinted in the *Daily Pennsylvanian,* February 1, 1961, pp. 3–5; and in the *Rosicrucian Digest,* February, 1962, pp. 67–75.

"The Freedom of the Juggernaut." *Mayo Clinic Proceedings,* January, 1965, pp. 7–21. Reprinted as "The Star Dragon," *Natural History,* June–July, 1970, pp. 18–26, 74–77; and in *Mineral Digest* 5 (Winter, 1973):47–58.

"Futures: The Crisis Animal." *Science Digest,* April, 1975, pp. 74–76.

"The Glory and Agony of Teaching." *Think,* October, 1962, pp. 22–25.

"The Gold Wheel." *Harper's,* August, 1971, pp. 68–71.

"The Great Deeps." *Harper's,* December, 1951, pp. 71–76.

"The Hope of Man." *New York Times,* November 6, 1972, p. 41.

"How Darwin Was Scooped." *Saturday Review,* September 6, 1958, p. 55.

"How Flowers Changed the World." *Saturday Review,* October 5, 1957, p. 49. Reprinted in *Science Digest,* February, 1959, pp. 70–75.

"I Too Would Go Out to the Manger." *Redbook,* December, 1968, pp. 31–33.

"The Illusion of the Two Cultures." *American Scholar* 33, no. 3 (Summer, 1964):387–99. Reprinted in *Rockefeller Institute Review* 2, no. 2 (March–April, 1964); *Sierra Club Bulletin,* December, 1964; and *Sunrise,* September and October, 1964 (two parts).

"In the Beginning Was the Artifact." *Saturday Review,* December 7, 1963, p. 52.

"Indian Mythology and Extinct Fossil Vertebrates." *American Anthropology* 47 (April, 1945):318–20.

"The Innocent Fox." *Natural History,* October, 1969, pp. 10–18.

"Instruments of Darkness." *Ameryka,* 1974, pp. 9–10.

"Is Man Alone in Space?" *Scientific American,* July, 1953, pp. 18, 80–82.

"Is Man Here to Stay?" *Scientific American,* November, 1950, pp. 52–55.

"The Island of the Great Stone Faces." *Holiday,* March, 1962, pp. 170–77.

"The Judgment of the Birds." *American Scholar* 25, no. 2 (Spring, 1956):151–60.

"Land Tenure in the Northeast: A Note on the History of a Concept." *American Anthropology* 49 (October, 1947):680–81.

"The Last Magician." *Playboy,* August, 1970, pp. 72, 138, 169–70. Reprinted in *National Parks and Conservation,* October, 1970, pp. 4–5; and as "The Sunflower Forest," *National Wildlife,* April–May, 1971, pp. 43–45.

"The Lesson of the Gull." *Reader's Digest,* May, 1979, pp. 183–84.

"Little Men and Flying Saucers." *Harper's,* March, 1953, pp. 86–91. Reprinted in *Nebraska Alumnus,* September, 1958, pp. 12–15, 31.

"Long Ago Man of the Future." *Harper's,* January, 1947, pp. 93–96.

"The Long Loneliness: Man and the Porpoise, Two Solitary Destinies." *Ameri-*

can Scholar 30, no. 1 (Winter, 1960–61):57–65.

"The Lost Nature Notebooks of Loren Eiseley." *Omni* 4, no. 9 (June 9, 1982):86–136.

"Madeline." *Pennsylvania Gazette,* December, 1975, pp. 26–29.

"Man in a Web." *Reader's Digest,* December, 1969, pp. 116–18.

"Man Is an Orphan of the Angry Winter." *Life,* February 16, 1968, pp. 76–87.

"Man the Fire-Maker." *Scientific American,* September, 1954, pp. 52–57.

"Man: The Lethal Factor." *American Scientist* 51, no. 1 (March, 1963):71–83: Reprinted as "The Lethal Factor," *Key Reporter,* Spring, 1963, pp. 1–3; and in *Pennsylvania Gazette,* June, 1963.

"The Man Who Saw Through Time." *Saturday Evening Post,* May 19, 1962, pp. 68–71.

"Mastodon and Early Man in America." *Science,* August 3, 1945, pp. 108–10.

"Men, Mastodons, and Myth." *Science Monthly* 62, supp. 3 (June, 1946):517–24.

"Missing Link or Hybrid—Which?" *Prairie Schooner* 20, no. 4 (Winter, 1946):250–56.

"Montagnais-Naskapi Bands and Family Hunting Districts of the Central and Southeastern Labrador Peninsula." *Proceedings of the American Philosophical Society* 85, no. 2 (January, 1942):215–42. With Frank G. Speck.

"The Most Perfect Day in the World." *Audubon,* November, 1975, pp. 32–35.

"Myth and Mammoth in Archeology." *American Antiquity* 11 (October, 1945):84–87.

"Nature, Man, and Miracles." *Horizon,* July, 1960, pp. 25–32. Reprinted in the *Episcopalian,* October, 1965, p. 58.

"Neanderthal Man and the Dawn of Human Paleontology." *Quarterly Review of Biology* 32 (December, 1957):323–29.

"A Neglected Anatomical Feature of the Foxhall Jaw." *Transactions of the Kansas Academy of Science* 46 (April, 1943):57–59.

"New Clue to the Missing Link." *Science Digest,* July, 1945, pp. 73–75.

"The Night the Shadows Whispered." *Reader's Digest,* May, 1968, pp. 139–40.

"No Secret Formula for Making Scientists." *New York Times Magazine,* October 18, 1964, pp. 66, 68, 74, 76.

"Obituary of a Bone Hunter." *Harper's,* October, 1947, pp. 325–29.

"Oreopithecus: Homunculus or Monkey?" *Scientific American,* June, 1956, pp. 91–100.

"Our Path Leads Upward." *Reader's Digest,* March, 1962, pp. 43–46.

"Paleontological Evidence for the Antiquity of the Scottsbluff Bison Quarry and Its Associated Artifacts." *American Anthropology* 37, no. 2 (April–June, 1935):306–19. With C. Bertrand Schultz.

"Paw Marks and Buried Towns." *American Scholar* 27, no. 2 (Spring, 1958):232–40.

"People Leave Skulls with Me." *Harper's,* May, 1951, pp. 43–49. Abridged in *Reader's Digest,* August, 1951, pp. 73–76.

"The Petrified Woman." *Reader's Digest*, March, 1972, pp. 137–41.

"The Places Below." *Harper's*, June, 1948, pp. 547–52.

"Poignant Work of Tampering with Prehistory." *Smithsonian*, October, 1975, pp. 34–40. Part of this piece first appeared as "Underground" in *Nebraska Alumnus*, October, 1937, pp. 10–11, 24.

"Pollen Analysis and Its Bearing Upon American Prehistory: A Critique." *American Antiquity* 5 (October, 1939):115–39.

"Post-Glacial Climatic Amelioration and the Extinction of *Bison taylori*." *Science*, June 26, 1942, pp. 646–47.

"Precisions Contradictoires sur l'âge de l'homme de Folsome." *L'Anthropologie*, 1938, p. 176.

"The Program on the Darwin Collection in the Library." *Proceedings of the American Philosophical Society* 98, no. 6 (December 23, 1954):449–52.

"Pseudo-Fossil Man." *Scientific American*, March, 1943, pp. 118–19.

"Racial and Phylogenetic Distinctions in the Intertemporal Interangular Index." *Transactions of the Kansas Academy of Science* 46 (1943):60–65.

"The Reception of the First Missing Links." *Proceedings of the American Philosophical Society* 98, no. 6 (December 23, 1954):453–65.

"Science and the Sense of the Holy." *Quest*, March, 1978, pp. 69–108.

"Science and the Unexpected Universe." *American Scholar* 35 (Summer, 1966):415–29.

"The Scientist as Prophet." *Harper's*, November, 1971, pp. 96–98.

"The Secret of Life." *Harper's*, October, 1953, pp. 64–68.

"Significance of Hunting Territory Systems of the Algonkian in Social Theory." *American Anthropology* 41 (April, 1939):269–80. With Frank G. Speck.

"The Skeleton in the Human Closet." *Saturday Review*, October 3, 1959, p. 20.

"The Snout." *Harper's*, September, 1950, pp. 88–92.

"Some Paleontological Inferences as to the Life Habits of the Australopithecenes." *Science*, July 16, 1943, p. 61.

"The Star Dragon." *Natural History*, June–July, 1970, pp. 18–26, 74–77. Reprinted in *Mineral Digest* 5 (Winter, 1973):47–58.

"The Star Thrower." *Oceans* 10 (September, 1977):54–57.

"The Sunflower Forest." *National Wildlife*, April–May, 1971, pp.43–45.

"There Came a Cry of Joy." *Reader's Digest*, March, 1977, pp. 97–99.

"There *Were* Giants." *Prairie Schooner* 19, no. 3 (Fall, 1945):189–93.

"There's Room For Doubt." *New York Times Book Review*, June 25, 1961, p. 4.

"Thoreau's Unfinished Business." *Natural History*, March, 1978, pp. 6–19.

"The Time of Man." *Horizon*, March, 1962, pp. 4–11.

"The Uncompleted Man." *Harper's*, March, 1964, pp. 51–54. Reprinted in *Graduate Journal, University of Texas*, Fall, 1964, pp. 257–63. Reprinted as "The Divine Animal," *Proceedings of the American Academy of Arts and Letters*, 2d ser. 14 (1964):333–41; and as "Instruments of Darkness," *Ameryka*, 1974, pp. 9–10.

"Underground." *Nebraska Alumnus*, October, 1937, pp. 10–11, 24. Reprinted

November–December, 1979, pp. 9–10.

"The Upheld Mirror." *National Education Association Journal,* December, 1963, p. 29.

"Using a Plague to Fight a Plague." *Saturday Review,* September 29, 1962, pp. 18–19, 34.

"Was Darwin Wrong About the Human Brain?" *Harper's,* November, 1955, pp. 66–70.

"Welcome to Craniology." *Harper's,* December, 1975, pp. 121–24.

"What Price Glory?: The Counterplaint of an Anthropologist." *American Social Review* 8 (December, 1943):635–37.

"Who Were Our Ancestors?: The Strange Tale of an Ancient Skull That Baffled a Committee of Experts Appointed to Investigate It." *Scientific American,* May, 1943, pp. 212–13.

"The Winter of Man." *New York Times,* January 16, 1972, p. 15. Reprinted as "The Ice Age of Fear Created by Modern Man," *Ottawa Journal,* January 29, 1972, p. 7.

3. Miscellaneous Prose

These selections represent books that Eiseley edited or volumes to which he contributed introductions or essays. The titles are arranged alphabetically.

An Appraisal of Anthropology Today. Chicago: University of Chicago Press, 1953. Coeditor.

"Charles Darwin, Rock Redondo: Science and Literature in the Galapagos." In *Galapagos: The Flow of Wildness.* Edited by Kenneth Brower. San Francisco: Sierra Club Books, 1970.

"The Creature from the Marsh." In *The Environment: Man on Trial.* Washington, D.C.: UNESCO, 1972.

Early Man in the Eden Valley, by John H. Moss and others. Philadelphia: University of Pennsylvania Museum, 1951. Editor.

"The Ethic of the Group." In *Social Control in a Free Society.* Edited by Robert Spitler. Philadelphia: University of Pennsylvania Press, 1960.

"Foreword" to *Not Man Apart: Lines from Robinson Jeffers.* Edited by David Brower. San Francisco: Sierra Club Books, 1965.

"Fossil Man and Human Evolution." In *Yearbook of Anthropology, 1955.* Edited by W. L. Thomas, Jr. Chicago: University of Chicago Press, 1956.

"Index Mollusca and Their Bearing on Certain Problems of Prehistory: A Critique." In *Twenty-Fifth Anniversary Studies of the Philadelphia Anthropological Society.* Philadelphia: University of Pennsylvania, 1937.

"The Intellectual Antecedents of the Descent of Man." In *Sexual Selection and the Descent of Man, 1871–1891.* Edited by Bernard Campbell. Chicago: Aldine Press, 1971.

"Introduction" to *The Forest and the Sea,* by Marston Bates. New York: Time, 1964.

"Introduction" to *On a Piece of Chalk,* by Thomas H. Huxley. New York: Charles Scribner's Sons, 1967.

"Introduction" to *The Shape of Likelihood: Relevance and the University.* Preface by Taylor Littleton. University: University of Alabama Press, 1971.

"The Lethal Factor." In *Science in Progress.* Edited by Wallace R. Brodi. New Haven: Yale University Press, 1964.

"Man." In *The Random House Encyclopedia.* New York: Random House, 1977.

"Man and Novelty." In *Time and Stratigraphy in the Evolution of Man.* Washington, D.C.: National Research Council, 1967.

"The Paleo-Indians: Their Survival and Diffusion." In *New Interpretations of Aboriginal American Culture History.* Washington, D.C.: Smithsonian Institution, 1955.

"Race Reflections of a Biological Historian." In *Science and the Concept of Race.* Edited by Margaret Mead, Theodosius Dobzhansky, Ethel Tobach, and Robert E. Light. New York: Columbia University Press, 1968.

"Space: The First Decade." In *Science Year: The World Book Annual, 1967.* Chicago: Field Enterprises Educational Corporation, 1967.

"Thoreau's Vision of the Natural World." In *The Illustrated World of Thoreau.* Edited by Howard Chapwick. New York: Grosset & Dunlop, 1974. Afterword.

4. Early Prose Pieces

"Autumn—A Memory." *Prairie Schooner* 1, no. 4 (October, 1927):238–39. Sketch.

"The Mop to K. C." *Prairie Schooner* 9, no. 1 (Winter, 1935):33–40. Short Story.

"Riding the Peddlers." *Prairie Schooner* 7, no. 1 (Winter, 1933):45–51. Narrative Sketch.

"Underground." *Nebraska Alumnus,* Ocotber, 1937, pp. 10–11, 24. Reprinted in *Nebraska Alumnus,* November–December, 1979, pp. 9–10. Sketch.

5. Early Reviews

"Bard of the Rustic Art." *Voices* 81 (April–May, 1935):44–46.

"Bibliana." *Prairie Schooner* 6, no. 2 (Spring, 1932):175.

"Bibliana." *Prairie Schooner* 7, no. 1 (Winter, 1933):73.

"Bibliana." *Prairie Schooner* 10, no. 2 (Summer, 1936):165.

"Bibliana." *Prairie Schooner* 10, no. 4 (Winter, 1936):315–16.

"Bibliana." *Prairie Schooner* 11, no. 1 (Spring, 1937):86.

"Music of the Mountain." *Voices* 67 (December–January, 1932–33):42–47.

"Stature Against the Earth." *Voices* 75 (April–May, 1934):53–56.

"Wings in the Wilderness." *Voices* 62 (February, 1932):153–54.
"World of Ruin." *Voices* 58 (Spring, 1931):39–41.

6. Poetry

Loren Eiseley was an active poet during two distinct periods in his career, from 1927 to 1945, and later from 1964 until his death. This alphabetized listing of his poetry publication spans both periods, and includes both collected and uncollected items. Eiseley often published his early poems in groups, and these are arranged according to the general title for the group. After 1972, some of these poems were reprinted from the volumes in which they first appeared.

The pseudonyms Eiseley used on a few of his early poems are also given.

"Against Cities." *Prairie Schooner* 4, no. 4 (Fall, 1930):252.
"Another Kind of Autumn." *Pennsylvania Gazette,* October, 1977, p. 33.
"The Beaver." *Audubon,* July, 1972, p. 77.
"Bleak Upland": "Against Lineage," "Upland Harvest," "Words to the Stoic," "Be Glad, You Worshippers." *Voices* 55 (April, 1930):158–60.
"Branch of Stone." *Midland* 19, no. 2 (March–April, 1932):34.
"The Cardinals." *Ladies' Home Journal,* November, 1972, p. 26.
"Cinquains": "Fear," "Despair," "Night in a Graveyard." *Prairie Schooner* 1, no. 4 (July, 1927):32. *Freshman Scrapbook.*
"Close Then the Heart." *Nebraska Alumnus,* January, 1936, p. 2.
"Coyote Country." *Midland* 19, no. 2 (March–April, 1932):49.
"Credo." *Prairie Schooner* 18, no. 3 (Fall, 1944):199.
"Death in Autumn." *Prairie Schooner* 1, no. 4 (October, 1927):245. Signed "Eronel Croye."
"Death Song for Two." *Prairie Schooner* 5, no. 4 (Fall, 1931):253.
"Deep in the Red Buttes." *University Review* (University of Kansas) 7, no. 3 (March, 1941):160.
"The Deer." *Audubon,* November, 1976, p. 75.
"The Deserted Homestead." *Poetry* 35, no. 111 (December, 1929):142–43.
"The Dollhouse." *Country Journal,* December, 1977, p. 112.
"Dusk Interval." *New York Herald-Tribune Books,* April 13, 1930, sec. 11, p. 8.
"Earthward." *Midland* 18, no. 2 (June, 1931):54.
"Epitaph." *American Scholar* 35 (Spring, 1966):292.
"Fabric for the Moth": "Fox Curse," "Word for the Frost," "Letter of Parting," "For the Tongueless," "Portrait." *Voices* 74 (February–March, 1934): 13–15.
"Fire in the Wind": "If He Hears no Sound," "Note at Midnight," "Sonnets for the Second Death," "Taste of Salt." *Voices* 69 (April–May, 1933):16–20.
"Fish at Paupack." *Audubon,* May, 1973, p. 31.
"Five Poems": "Hill Orchard in Spring," "Last Headland," "Out of This Crystal," "Compound," "Masked Dance: Night Club." *Voices* 85 (Spring, 1936):30–32.

"Flight 857." *Expedition* 15, no. 1 (Fall, 1972):9.

"For a Lost Home." *Prairie Schooner* 5, no. 2 (Spring, 1931):157.

"Four Poems": "Words for Forgetting," "Return to White Mountain," "Poem to Accompany a Poem," "Incident in the Zoo." *Prairie Schooner* 8, no. 3 (Summer, 1934):118–20.

"Four Poems": "The Buzzards," "Mars," "Dreamed in a Dark Millennium," "The Shore Hunters." *Harper's,* June, 1977, p. 57.

"Fox Curse." *Literary Digest,* May 19, 1934, p. 35. See also "Fabric for the Moth."

"Fox Way." *The General Magazine and Historical Chronicle* (University of Pennsylvania) 39 (January, 1937):191.

"Graveyard Studies": "Daguerreotype on a Tombstone," "A Sunken Grave," "The Santa Fe Trail." *Prairie Schooner* 1, no. 4 (October, 1927):268. Signed "Silas Amon."

"The Hawk." *American Scholar* 34 (Summer, 1965):370.

"How Brief Upon the Wind." *Science Digest,* September, 1977, p. 82.

"Incident in the Zoo." *Literary Digest,* November 10, 1934, p. 32. See also "Four Poems."

"The Innocent Assassins." *Audubon,* November, 1973, pp. 88–89.

"Knossus." *Poetry* 128, no. 6 (September, 1976):347–48.

"The Last Gold Penny." *Prairie Schooner* 2, no. 4 (Fall, 1928):242.

"Last Wing." *Literary Digest,* June 22, 1935, p. 25. Reprinted in *Voices* 81 (April–May, 1935):16.

"Leaving September." *American Mercury,* September, 1936, p. 90.

"Let The Red Fox Run." *Ladies' Home Journal,* June, 1964, p. 98c.

"London." *Audubon,* May, 1974, pp. 46–47.

"Night Snow." *Prairie Schooner* 2, no. 4 (Winter, 1928):57. Signed "Tlo Honda."

"Nocturne for Autumn's Ending." *Prairie Schooner* 7, no. 4 (Fall, 1933):165.

"Nocturne for Crickets and Men." In *Best College Verse.* Edited by Jessie Rehder. New York: Harper and Brothers, 1931, p. 62.

"Nocturne in Silver." *American Poetry Journal,* March, 1935, p. 15.

"Now in This Drowsy Moment." *Prairie Schooner* 10, no. 4 (Winter, 1936):251.

"October Has the Heart." *Prairie Schooner* 15, no. 3 (Fall, 1941):151. Reprinted in *The Best Poems of 1942.* Edited by Thomas Moult. London: Jonathan Cope, 1943, p. 55.

"One Remembering the Marshes." *Prairie Schooner* 4, no. 2 (Spring, 1930):78–80.

"The Poet Surveys His Garden." *Midland* 16, no. 3 (May–June, 1930):159.

"Poison Oak." *Prairie Schooner* 3, no. 4 (Fall, 1929):247. Reprinted in *Poems by Nebraska Poets* 1 (1940–41):57.

"The Quainter Dust." *Prairie Schooner* 3, no. 2 (Spring, 1929):160.

"Safe in the Toy Box." *Poetry* 128, no. 6 (September, 1976):345–46.

"Say It Thus with the Heart." *Prairie Schooner* 16, no. 1 (Spring, 1942):23.

"A Serpent's Eye." *Audubon,* July, 1973, pp. 24–25.

"Six Poems": "Last Wing," "Things Will Go," "Now the Singing Is Done,"
    "On the Pecos Dunes," "So With the Heart," "Song Without Logic."
    Voices 81 (April–May, 1935):16–19.

"The Snowstorm." *Audubon,* January, 1976, pp. 2–3.

"Song for the Wolf's Coat." *Voices* 71 (August–September, 1933):26.

"Sonnet." *Prairie Schooner* 9, no. 4 (Fall, 1935):242.

"Sonnet for Age." *New York Herald-Tribune Books,* June 15, 1930, sec. 11, p. 6.

"Sparrow Hawk Resting." *Audubon,* March, 1977, pp. 48–49.

"Spiders." *Prairie Schooner* 2, no. 2 (Spring, 1928):92–93.

"Spring in This Town." *Midland* 19, nos. 2–3 (March–June, 1933):42.

"Star Cycles." *Southwest Review* 16, no. 2 (January, 1931):264.

"The Striders." *Audubon,* September, 1972, p. 29.

"Susu the Dolphin." *Oceans* 12 (Summer, 1979):33.

"Tasker's Farm." *Midland* 16, no. 4 (July–August, 1930):182–84.

"There Is No Peace." *Prairie Schooner* 1, no. 4 (July, 1927):11. *Freshman
    Scrapbook.*

"These Are the Stars." *Prairie Schooner* 12, no. 1 (Spring, 1938):17.

"Three Poems": "Prairie Spring," "Never Like Deer," "The Fishers." *Prairie
    Schooner* 15, no. 1 (Spring 1941):51–52. Reprinted in *Niagara Falls
    Gazette,* August 23, 1941, p. 12.

"To the Furred and Feathered." *Poems by Nebraska Poets* 2 (1942–43):23.

"Toward Winter." *Voices* 57 (Winter, 1931):274.

"The Trout." *Prairie Schooner* 19, no. 4 (Winter, 1945):323.

"Two Hours From Now." *Poetry* 130, no. 1 (April, 1977):33.

"Two Poems": "Brief Song," "Night Wakening." *Voices* 64 (April, 1932):240.

"Two Poems": "Tasting the Mountain Spring," "The Spider." *Poetry* 54, no. 7
    (September, 1939):316–17.

"*Warning to Lovers.*" *New York Herald-Tribune Books,* January 26, 1930, p. 6.

"Waste." *Bozart* 2, no. 4 (March–April, 1929):12.

"We Are the Scriveners." *Defenders,* October, 1978, p. 249.

"Whisper Behind a Guide at the Cliff House." *Midland* 19, no. 4 (July–
    August, 1932):85.

"Wind Child." *Audubon,* May, 1977, p. 20.

"Winter Sign." *Prairie Schooner* 17, no. 3 (Fall, 1943):163.

"Winter Visitant." *Prairie Schooner* 17, no. 4 (Winter, 1943):218.

"Words on a Spring Road." *Prairie Schooner* 9, no. 3 (Summer, 1935):186.

SECONDARY SOURCES

No comprehensive bibliography of Loren Eiseley's work has yet been published,
although an official bibliography is being prepared for the University of
Pennsylvania Archives.

1. Books

Haydn, Hiram. *Words and Faces.* New York: Harcourt, Brace, Jovanovich, 1974. Haydn's publishing memoir contains recollections of his experiences as Eiseley's editor at the *American Scholar,* Random House, Atheneum Press, and Harcourt, Brace, Jovanovich. Good discussion of Eiseley's relations with his publishers.

Mangione, Jerre. *The Dream and the Deal: The Federal Writers' Project, 1935–43.* Boston: Little, Brown & Co., 1972. Includes a valuable discussion of Eiseley's work in 1935 with the Nebraska WPA Writers' project.

2. Critical Articles

Auden, W. H. "Concerning the Unpredictable." *New Yorker,* February 21, 1970, pp. 118–25. The best general appreciation of Eiseley's writing, this first appeared as a review of *The Unexpected Universe,* and was later used as the introduction to *The Star Thrower.* Interprets Eiseley's interpolated anecdotes in his essays as examples of "numinous encounters." Good discussion of Eiseley's nonsectarian religious sensibility.

Carlisle, E. Fred. "The Heretical Science of Loren Eiseley." *Centennial Review* 18 (Fall, 1974):354–77. Sound discussion of Eiseley's appropriation of scientific insights for literary purposes and their metaphoric use in his writing. Defends Eiseley's reputation as a literary naturalist and shows how his works have transformed biology and have given it a new "popular" idiom.

————. "The Poetic Achievement of Loren Eiseley." *Prairie Schooner* 51, no. 2 (Summer, 1977):111–29. Excellent overview and critical discussion of Eiseley's early poetry. Examines the "fugitive persona" in Eiseley's poetry and discusses his development as a poet, from the early verse to *The Innocent Assassins.*

Nemerov, Howard. "Loren Eiseley: 1907–1977." *Proceedings of the American Academy of Arts and Letters* 2, no. 29 (1978):77–81. Perceptive memorial tribute with useful comments on Eiseley's later poetry and his influence on Nemerov's career.

Schwartz, James M. "Loren Eiseley: The Scientist as Literary Artist." *Georgia Review* 31 (Winter, 1977):855–71. Important discussion of Eiseley's "undervalued literary achievements." Examines the thematic progression of Eiseley's most important works and demonstrates their unity.

Umland, Rudolph. "Lowry Wimberly and Others: Recollections of a Beerdrinker." *Prairie Schooner* 51, no. 1 (Spring, 1977):17–51. Valuable recollection of Eiseley as an undergraduate at the University of Nebraska and as a member of the early *Prairie Schooner* staff. Discusses Wimberly's influence on Eiseley, Mari Sandoz, and other students of his who later became writers.

Werkley, Caroline E. "Lost Pumas, Pincushions, and Gypsies." *Journal of Library History* 11 (October, 1976):343–53. Detailed discussion of

Eiseley's lifelong book-buying and collecting habits. Offers some fascinating reflections on his range of reading and intellectual interests.

————. "Of Skulls, Spiders and Small Libraries." *Wilson Library Bulletin* 44 (October, 1969): 188–96. Detailed discussion of the holdings in Eiseley's personal library, along with an amusing description of his old tower office at the University Museum. Provides additional discussion of Eiseley's reading tastes and his passion for book collecting.

————. "Professor Cope, Not Alive But Well." *Smithsonian,* August, 1975, pp. 72–75. Fascinating account of how Eiseley came to acquire the remains of Professor Edward Drinker Cope, a noted nineteenth-century paleontologist. Offers an interesting contrast with an anecdote in "Barbed Wire and Brown Skulls," in *The Night Country.*

3. Interviews

"A Conversation with Loren Eiseley on Ego and Evolution." *Psychology Today,* October, 1970, pp. 75–96. Editor Robert Glasgow interviews Eiseley on the history of science, man's changing concept of time, and the public reception of Darwinism. A valuable discussion of the "dichotomy between religion and science" and the scientist's difficulty in believing in God.

"The Immense Journey of Loren Eiseley." *Esquire,* March, 1967, pp. 92–94, 44–50. Perhaps the most useful in-depth interview with Eiseley. John Mandelman offers a thorough summary and assessment of Eiseley's career and accomplishments.

"Loren Eiseley." *Publisher's Weekly,* November 3, 1975, pp. 10–12. An interview that appeared at the time *All the Strange Hours* was published, in which Eiseley reviews his career and discusses his reasons for writing an autobiography.

"Loren Eiseley's Immense Journey." *Today/The Philadelphia Inquirer,* January 27, 1974, pp. 16–20. A valuable extended interview that offers an excellent biographical introduction to Eiseley's career. Eiseley elaborates here on many personal incidents mentioned in his books and essays, which Bob Lancaster has rearranged in chronological order. He traces the genesis of Eiseley's literary interests to his solitary childhood.

"Notes on a Lifetime of Probing the Unusual," *Christian Science Monitor,* February 11, 1976, pp. 14–15. An interview granted at the time Eiseley's autobiography was published. He discusses his autobiography as "a continuation of his personal essays," and expresses his dissatisfaction with the limitations of the scientific world view, offering instead a glimpse of his personal beliefs.

4. Selected Reviews

Bates, Marston. *"Darwin's Century." Science,* June 27, 1958, pp. 1493–94. Lucid discussion of how Eiseley traces the "Darwinian revolution" from the earlier "Copernican revolution" in astronomy. Bates calls the book "an important contribution" to the history of ideas.

Bradbury, Ray. "240 Page Poem of Simmering Life Vibrations." *Los Angeles Times Book Review,* December 12, 1971, pp. 1, 3. A warm tribute to Eiseley by a science-fiction writer whom he influenced. Bradbury praises the poetic qualities of *The Night Country*.

Buettner-Janusch, John. *"The Firmament of Time." American Anthropologist* 65 (1963):693–94. An example of the kind of negative response Eiseley's writing elicited from some of his materialistically minded scientific colleagues.

Cooke, Michael G. "The Hero in Autobiography." *Yale Review* 65 (June, 1976):587–93. An interesting theoretical discussion of the autobiographical persona in *All the Strange Hours* and an attempt to relate Eiseley's book to current trends in autobiography.

Deevey, Edward. "Man and Nature: Retrospect and Prospect." *Yale Review* 50 (Autumn, 1960):120–22. Appreciative appraisal of *The Firmament of Time* and Marston Bates's *The Forest and the Sea* as works of humanistic science.

Dobzhansky, Theodosius. *"The Unexpected Universe." American Anthropologist* 73 (1971):305–6. Praises the imaginative qualities of *The Unexpected Universe,* calling Eiseley "a Proust miraculously turned into an evolutionary biologist."

Dubos, Rene. *"The Invisible Pyramid." Smithsonian,* November, 1970, pp. 70–71. In his laudatory review, Dubos observes that "Eiseley's style and images create a mood of awe and wonderment which fits his approach to the human condition."

Gould, Stephen Jay. "Darwin Vindicated!" *New York Review of Books,* August 16, 1979, pp. 36–38. An even-handed review of *Darwin and the Mysterious Mr. X* in which Gould questions Eiseley's claim that Darwin "borrowed" the concept of natural selection from Edward Blyth without proper acknowledgement.

Greene, John C. *"Darwin's Century." American Anthropologist* 61 (1959):519–22. Useful summary of Eiseley's arguments in *Darwin's Century* by a fellow historian of science.

Gruber, Howard E. "The Origin of the *Origin of Species." New York Times Book Review,* July 22, 1979, pp. 7, 16. A rather harsh and polemical review attacking the substance of Eiseley's arguments in *Darwin and the Mysterious Mr. X.* Perhaps the most unfavorable review of this book.

Howard, Ben. "Comment." *Poetry,* 126 (April, 1975):44–46. Howard offers some useful comments on the weaknesses in Eiseley's poetic style in this review of *The Innocent Assassins.*

Irvine, William. "Evolution of the Theory." *New York Times Book Review,* June 29, 1958, p. 4. Useful summary of Eiseley's arguments in *Darwin's Century* by a respected Victorian scholar.

Kottler, Malcolm Jay. "Eiseley on Darwin." *Bioscience* 30 (July, 1980):478. Negative review of *Darwin and the Mysterious Mr. X.* Kottler labels Eiseley's thesis as "untenable."

Krutch, Joseph Wood. "The Tortuous Road to Knowledge." *Saturday Review,* August 20, 1960, pp. 21–22. Of *The Firmament of Time,* Krutch remarks that "it is doubtful if anyone ever said more on so large a subject in so short a compass."

Novak, Michael. *"The Unexpected Universe."* *Psychology Today* 4 (June, 1970):4–6. Relates Eiseley's capacity for wonder to his midwest rearing in this perceptive review of *The Unexpected Universe.*

Olney, James J. *"All the Strange Hours."* *New Republic,* November 1, 1975, pp. 30–34. The most perceptive review of Eiseley's autobiography. Olney relates the book to the practice of autobiography and praises its elegiac qualities.

Prescott, Orville. "Books of the Times." *New York Times,* December 27, 1957, p. 17. Important early review of *The Immense Journey* that marked the beginning of the book's slow critical reception.

Ross, Nancy Wilson. "Dr. Eiseley's Universe." *American Scholar* 40, no. 1 (Winter, 1970–71):38–39. Useful discussion of the major themes and the religious implications of *The Unexpected Universe.*

Sinnott, Edmund W. "The Life Sciences and the General Reader." *Yale Review* 51, no. 1 (Autumn, 1961):165–74. Appreciative review of *Darwin's Century* and other biological books written for the general reader.

Stahlman, William D. *"The Unexpected Universe."* *Saturday Review,* December 13, 1969, pp. 38–40. Useful discussion of Eiseley's metaphoric style, which Stahlman calls "science in a humanistic language."

Whittemore, Reed. "Two Poets." *New Republic,* December 2, 1972, pp. 22–23. Prefers the poems of A. R. Ammons to those of Eiseley in *Notes of an Alchemist,* which he feels strain after significance.

5. Dissertations, Theses, and Articles

Appel, George F. *Modern Masters and Archaic Motifs of the Animal Poem.* Ph.D. dissertation, University of Minnesota, 1973. A valuable discussion in chapter 8 of the shamanistic motif in Eiseley's animal poems.

Umland, Rudolph. "Looking Back at the Wimberly Years." Manuscript. Author's copy. Valuable retrospective appraisal of the influence of Professor Lowry Wimberly and the *Prairie Schooner* staff on the subsequent literary careers of Eiseley and other Lincoln writers. The article also contains some useful biographical information on Eiseley's college years at the University of Nebraska.

Werkley, Caroline E. "The Old Bones Man: Report of the Barlow File." Manuscript. University of Pennsylvania Archives. Fascinating account of the role Eiseley played in arranging the transfer of F. O. Barlow's casts of early human fossil remains from London to the University of Pennsylvania.

————. "Report of Loren Eiseley Collection/July, 1978." Manuscript. University of Pennsylvania Archives. Comprehensive introduction to and description of the Loren Eiseley papers prepared for the University of Pennsylvania Archives.

————. "Report of Loren Eiseley Collection/Revised, September, 1978." Manuscript. University of Pennsylvania Archives. Update of the original report, with a slightly different focus. Both versions are useful to the Eiseley scholar.

Index